Can You Believe It?

Stories and Idioms from Real Life

Book 3

D1567536

Jann Huizenga
Linda Huizenga

OXFORD

UNIVERSITY PRESS

Oxford University Press
198 Madison Avenue
New York, NY 10016 USA

Great Clarendon Street
Oxford OX2 6DP England

Oxford New York

*Athens Auckland Bangkok Bogotá Buenos Aires
Cape Town Chennai Dar es Salaam Delhi
Florence Hong Kong Istanbul Karachi Kolkata
Kuala Lumpur Madrid Melbourne Mexico City
Mumbai Nairobi Paris São Paulo Shanghai
Singapore Taipei Tokyo Toronto Warsaw*

and associated companies in
Berlin Ibadan

OXFORD is a trademark of Oxford University Press.

ISBN 0-19-437276-6

Copyright © 2000 Oxford University Press

No unauthorized photoocpying.

Editorial Manager: Janet Aitchison
Editor: Lynne Barsky
Production Editor: Klaus Jekeli
Design Manager: Lynne Torrey
Designer: Gail de Luca
Senior Art Buyer: Patricia Marx
Art Buyer and Photo Researcher: Laura Nash
Production Manager: Shanta Persaud

Printing (last digit): 10 9 8 7 6 5 4 3

Printed in Hong Kong

Acknowledgments

Illustrations by Patrick Merrell, Wally Niebert, Tom Powers, William Waitzman

Cover illustration by Ken Condon

Location and studio photography by Susan Shapelle

The publishers would like to thank the following for their permission to reproduce photographs: Fernandez & Peck, Ned Gillette/Adventure Film & Photo; Allsport; John Cancalosi, S.J. Krasemann, Richard Weiss/Peter Arnold; Robin Bowman; Colonial Williamsburg; Steve Nehf/Denver Post; Rick Souders/Foodpix; David Fukomoto; Jules' Underwater Lodge; Tom Sweeney/Minneapolis-St. Paul Star Tribune; Shane Young/NYT Pictures; Providence Journal; Rob Meyers/Quokka.com; Rod Flemming/Scotscape; Tim Hynds/Sioux City Journal; Solar Survival Architecture; Stock Market; Shaun Walker

Credits
The stories in this book have been adapted from the following material: **p.** 2: *The New York Times* (and *The Associated Press*), January 7, 1999; **p.** 7: *The Spokesman-Review,* March 26, 1993; **p.** 8: *The Associated Press,* June 1, 1998; **p.** 13: *The Associated Press,* April 13, 1999; **p.** 14: *The New Mexican* (and *The Associated Press*), March 2, 1998; **p.** 20: *Outside,* May, 1998; *The Associated Press,* May 28, 1998; *Public Eye with Bryant Gumble* (CBS TV special), July 1998; *www.mountainvisions.com/Everest/everest2.html;* **p.** 26: *Missoulian,* August 1 and 2, 1998; **p.** 31: *Missoulian,* July 30, 1998; **p.** 32: *People,* December 21, 1998; **p.** 37: *Six Drown Saving Chicken and Other True Stories from the Reuters 'Oddly Enough' File,* Reuters, 1996; **p.** 38: *The Providence Journal,* December 22, 1998; **p.** 50: *Reuters,* October 22, 1998; **p.** 55: *Reuters,* February 25, 1999; **p.** 56: *Minneapolis-St. Paul Star Tribune,* June 6, 1998; **p.** 61: *The Associated Press,* August 3, 1998; **p.** 62: *The Albuquerque Journal,* July 18, 1998; **p.** 68: *U.S. News & World Report,* March 4, 1996 and January 12, 1998; **p.** 85: *The New Mexican* (and *The Associated Press*), February 14, 1999; **p.** 86: *The New Mexican* (and *The Associated Press*), February 7, 1999; **p.** 91: *Reader's Digest,* November, 1998

The publishers would also like to thank the following business and persons:

Jules' Undersea Lodge, 51 Shoreland Drive, Key Largo, Florida 33037, for their contribution to the story on page 74.

Figen and Dan Haigh for their graciousness in accepting to be interviewed and photographed for the story on page 80.

For our parents,
Dolly and John,
who gave us a love of language.

To the Student

In this book you will enjoy learning everyday idiomatic American English through amazing true stories from around the world.

When you study vocabulary, it is not enough to learn individual words. Everyday English is filled with expressions that are two or more words long, such as *live through, go out on a limb,* and *on the house*. These expressions are essential to successful communication in English, and they need to be learned as individual units, in the same way as individual words. In this book you will find **idioms, fixed expressions** and **phrasal verbs**.

What is an idiom?

An **idiom** is a group of words that has a meaning different from the meaning of its individual parts. In the example below, you probably know all the individual words, but you still may not understand the meaning of the expressions. This is because the expressions are idiomatic.

> **Drop me a line** if you **break new ground** in the experiment!

Drop me a line means *write me a short letter,* and *break new ground* means *do something that has not been done before.*

What is a fixed expression?

Be enthusiastic about, take a bath, and *year after year* are **fixed expressions.** You will understand the whole expression if you know the meaning of the parts. But the translation of a fixed expression into your language may not be word for word.

What is a phrasal verb?

A **phrasal verb** is a verb followed by a particle such as *in, at, on, for, out, about,* etc. *Find out* and *search for* are phrasal verbs. *Find out* means *discover,* and *search for* means *try hard to find*. Phrasal verbs are usually idiomatic. You can learn more about phrasal verbs in Appendix D, page 111.

The steps to learning idioms in this book are as follows:

1. **Read quickly** to get the main idea.
2. **Listen to the story** several times while you look at pictures to get used to the idioms.
3. **Read the story** again and study the idioms.
4. **Listen** and **complete** the idioms.
5. **Match the idioms** with their definitions.
6. **Tell the story** using the idioms while looking only at pictures.
7. **Talk about the story** and then about yourself using the idioms.
8. **Take a dictation** that uses the idioms.
9. **Complete the idioms** in new sentences.
10. **Look at the grammar** of some of the idioms.
11. **Write a dialogue** using the unit idioms and **act it out**.
12. **Review the idioms** by filling in the blanks in a new story or dialogue.

Extra study aids include:

- A listening cassette
- **Appendix A:** An answer key (page 98)
- **Appendix B:** Dictations (page 102)
- **Appendix C:** An appendix that groups the idioms in the book in various ways to help you remember their form and meaning (page 104)
- **Appendix D:** An appendix that explains the grammar of phrasal verbs (page 111) and lists the phrasal verbs that appear in this book (page 112)
- **Lexicon:** A list of all the idioms in the book with definitions, examples, language notes, and idiomatic synonyms and antonyms (page 116).

To the Teacher

A General Introduction

The goal of *Can You Believe It? Book 3* is to teach high frequency idioms, phrasal verbs, and fixed expressions in the context of true, memorable stories to ESL/EFL students at an intermediate level. It is founded on two basic premises: 1) that everyone loves a good story, and 2) that vocabulary acquisition occurs more readily when new items are embedded in engaging, whole contexts and used in tasks that have meaning and purpose. The book is written for classroom use, but will also work well for self-study when used with the audio program.

Thanks in part to Michael Lewis's influential work on lexical issues, TESOL professionals are increasingly aware that idioms and fixed expressions form a significant part of the lexicon of English and are central to natural language use. These prefabricated multi-word expressions must be acquired as wholes in the same way as individual words. *Can You Believe It? Book 3* teaches the following kinds of high-frequency fixed lexical expressions:

- traditional, graphic idioms, such as *hungry as a bear, follow the crowd,* and *go out on a limb;*

- non-traditional idioms, such as *spend time doing something, have got to,* and *globe-trotting;*

- two- or three-word adverbial chunks, such as *by mistake, according to,* and *at present;*

- two- or three-word phrasal verbs, such as *come up, put up with* and *back off;* and,

- common expressions consisting of de-lexicalized verbs, such as *make* or *get* plus a noun or adjective (*make history, get together*), word partnerships that are likely to produce translation mistakes and need to be learned as chunks.

Can You Believe It? Book 3 is compatible with comprehension approaches such as *The Natural Approach.* The picture sequences that correspond to the stories provide the basis for great "comprehensible input." Hence, the book can be used for listening comprehension and general language acquisition at intermediate levels as well as for the specific mastery of idioms and expressions.

The approach thoroughly integrates the four skills of listening, reading, speaking, and writing. Activities are sequenced so that input precedes output. The initial activities rely heavily on listening and use picture sequences as visual supports for comprehension. It is through this richly contextualized (and repeated) listening that students begin to make hypotheses about the new expressions and develop a feel for their use. Students then go on to read the story—an essential step that will provide welcome written reinforcement for visually oriented learners and will help all students with their literacy skills. After students' pumps have been primed, so to speak, with the listening and reading input, they are ready to begin producing the idioms in speaking and writing. The output activities become progressively more demanding; these include story retelling, thought-provoking personal questions, dictation, personalized sentence completions, and dialogue production.

Researchers contend that we acquire new lexical items by meeting them a number of times (seven times, some say). Thus, in *Can You Believe It? Book 3,* students will revisit the idioms and expressions many times within each unit as well as in review units and, to some extent, from unit to unit. (The idioms that are recycled between units are listed in the Table of Contents as well as in The New Idioms and Expressions box which follows each reading.)

Extra Features

Listening Cassette
The cassette features dramatic readings of all the stories and provides the **Dictations** for each unit (see **Appendix B**). The stories are read by different actors with varying voices and styles so students are exposed to language variety.

Answer Key (Appendix A)
Students who use the book independently will especially appreciate this feature, though classroom teachers will also find it handy.

Idiom Groups (Appendix C)
This appendix is a rich resource for those students who would like a better sense of how the idioms in *Can You Believe It? Book 3* can be grouped together semantically.

Phrasal Verbs (Appendix D)
Simple but detailed grammar explanations of phrasal verbs are included here for students who feel ready for this information.

Lexicon
The Lexicon gives extra information about each idiom and fixed expression in the book. Definitions, additional examples, grammar information, more collocations, and idiomatic synonyms and antonyms are included.

Specific Teaching Suggestions
The exercises and activities in each unit can be used in a variety of ways, and you are encouraged to experiment and adapt them as you see fit. The suggested sequence can be changed, depending on your goals and your specific class needs.

1. Quick Reading
Before students read the story quickly to get the gist, have them do one of the following prediction activities:

> a. Cover the story and look at the picture sequence on the opposite page. Discuss (in pairs or small groups) what the story seems to be about.

> b. Cover the story. Look at the title and the picture on the story page. Make predictions about the story.

Then ask students to read the story quickly just to get the main idea or the basic story line. You might give them a time limit for this. (The details of the story will become clear during Exercise 2 as they listen to it repeatedly while looking at the picture sequence.) Previewing the story in this manner will allow students—especially those who are stronger visual than oral/aural learners—to relax and better comprehend the story and the new idioms in context during the listening "input" stage. It is best to have students read silently at this stage since they will want to process the text in their own way.

2. Listen
Ask students to cover the story. Play the cassette or, if you prefer, read the story to the students. If you are not using the cassette, be sure to say the numbers as you move from picture to picture so students can follow (at least during the first listening). Tell the story at a natural speed, pausing somewhat longer than usual at the end of breath groups and sentences. This will give students important processing time. The goal of this activity is to provide students with truly "comprehensible input," i.e., an acquisition stage in which a high degree of contextualization will allow them to formulate hypotheses and discover meaning in language they are hearing for the first time. Making inferences and hypotheses about new language in context is a skill that all language learners need to feel comfortable with; this exercise thus develops good learning strategies while helping students acquire new language. During a second or third telling of the story, you may want to write the new idioms on the board, as reinforcement for your visually oriented students. (The easiest thing would be to write them on the board prior to the retelling and point to them as they occur.)

As an assessment technique (to see how well students have understood and internalized the new expressions in the story), tell students you are going to talk about the pictures out of order. They should point to the picture you are describing. Or, as an alternative, retell the story making some major "mistakes." Have students signal somehow (by raising their hands, making a face, or make a buzzing sound) when they hear a mistake.

3. Read the Story

Your more visual learners will be especially eager to take a closer look at the story at this point, double-checking their hypotheses with the New Idioms and Expressions box. After students have had some silent time for re-reading, you might want to have them read aloud for pronunciation practice. Volunteers could take turns reading to the whole class, or pairs could read to each other, helping each other with pronunciation. You may want to do part or all of Exercise 6 at this point (see suggestions below).

For a bit of extra practice with the idioms, and as a good lead-in to Exercise 4, you could conduct the following matching activity: Write the unit idioms on slips of paper or index cards. Cut the idioms in half. Give a half to each student. Tell students to stand up, walk around the room, and find the other half of their idiom. As a check, have the pairs say their idioms aloud to the whole class.

4. Listen and Complete

This is an oral exercise. Students listen to the story. The tape pauses in the middle of each idiom for a few seconds, allowing students to call out the second half of the idiom. If you do not use the tape, and are reading the story to students, pause after the first part of the idiom and let students call out the rest.

5. Match

This activity functions as an assessment of sorts, ensuring that students (a) can put the parts of the idioms together and (b) understand their meanings before they have to use the idioms in the story-retelling activity in Exercise 6. As an alternative to this activity, give each student a card on which half of an idiom has been written, and ask them to mingle with their classmates to find their "match."

6. Tell the Story

At this point, the exercises move away from recognition into production. Elicit the story orally from the whole class first. Encourage students to call out the ideas of the story in chronological order. They can, of course, look at the picture sequence during this activity, but the story should be covered. The retelling will be a paraphrase of the original story, but students will probably reuse most of the new idioms. (You could have the idioms listed on the board to give students a bit of extra help). You may want to run this activity as a variation on *Language Experience,* writing down sentences and phrases on the board as students suggest them. Underlining the idioms and fixed expressions that students generate will help to highlight them.

Next, ask students to work in pairs or small groups to retell the story to each other. Once again, make sure they cover the story. One way for them to work is with *Talking Chips,* communication regulators used in *Cooperative Learning.* Working in pairs or groups of three, each student takes four or five *Talking Chips* (e.g., tokens, such as buttons, poker chips, or paint chips). Together, they reconstruct the story. As each student contributes a sentence, he or she puts in a token. (The chips ensure that each student speaks and that all have an equal opportunity to participate.)

7. Answer the Questions

The questions in this section either use an idiom from the unit or elicit one in the answer. As an alternative to the traditional whole-class-question-answer technique here, you might want to try using *Numbered Heads Together,* a *Cooperative Learning* activity.

The steps to *Numbered Heads Together* are as follows:

a. Students get into teams of four and number off from one to four.

b. The teacher asks a question.

c. Students on each team literally put their heads together and reach a consensus on the answer and the phrasing of the answer.

d. The teacher calls a number at random. Students with that number raise their hands (or stand up) and report on their team's answer. You will probably want to get each team's answer, as there will be variations to discuss and comment on.

The advantages of this questioning technique over the traditional whole-class-question-answer technique are the following: all students are involved since no one knows who will be called on; stronger students help weaker ones; students have "think time" and "rehearsal time" in small groups before they have to respond in front of the whole class; and a wrong response is not so embarrassing because it comes from a team rather than an individual.

The "About You" questions can be answered orally, either in a whole class setting or in small groups. These questions are also good springboards for paragraph writing. Allow students to choose their favorite ones to respond to, and to share their writing with partners.

8. Take a Dictation
Play the cassette or use **Appendix B** to read students the dictation. A recommended procedure is as follows:

a. Read the dictation once at normal speed. Students should not write at this stage.

b. Read the dictation again, this time pausing long enough after each breath group or sentence for students to write.

c. Read the dictation a third time, at near-normal speed, allowing students to check their writing.

Students can correct their own work or the work of a partner using **Appendix B.** Students might also like to try peer dictation, where one student dictates to another.

9. Complete the Idioms
This exercise introduces completely new contexts in which students have to produce the unit idioms. (They should not have to look back at the New Idioms box at this point.)

10. Look at Grammar
This section deals in depth with three or four of the unit idioms and draws attention to the types of words and phrases which can follow the idioms, or, in the case of phrasal verbs, to their special grammatical properties. Students may check the Lexicon on pages 116-150 for grammatical information on other idioms not treated here. The sentence completions in this section ask students to write true, personal sentences. Students can share their sentences in small groups, and you might ask volunteers to put their sentences on the board afterwards. Be sure that the volunteers understand that their contributions may need correction!

11. Write a Dialogue
This activity encourages students to produce the unit idioms in creative and novel contexts. It asks students to work in pairs to write short dialogues, using at least four unit idioms. Give students time in pairs not only to create the dialogues, but also to rehearse them (and, ideally, to memorize them). Depending on the time you can devote to this activity, you may want to have pairs perform for other pairs and then for the whole class, or you may want to simply call on a few volunteers to perform for the class. If you can keep a small stash of props (hats, scarves, sunglasses, and other odd items) available for this activity and ask students to use some props as well as appropriate body language as they perform, this task will be greatly enlivened.

12. Complete the Dialogue or Story
.After students work individually, in pairs, or in groups to fill in the blanks with the appropriate expressions from the box, they can check their answers in **Appendix A.**

Six of the fourteen units have a dialogue exercise. Students can practice the dialogue in pairs, perhaps preparing for an expressive reading of the dialogue for the whole class.

The remaining eight units have a story exercise. After filling in the blanks, students can either practice reading the story to each other in pairs or paraphrase it to each other, being sure to use the idioms from the box in the retelling.

Acknowledgments

Many people contributed to *Can You Believe It? Book 3*, and we're grateful to them all. Susan Lanzano at Oxford University Press was the guiding light from start to finish. Lynne Barsky was a generous and patient editor whose care and expertise made this a much better book. Janet Aitchison was a moving force in the insightful resolution of many problems. Special thanks to Klaus Jekeli, production editor, and to the design team including Lynne Torrey, Gail de Luca, Trish Marx, and Laura Nash. Good friend and colleague Ken Sheppard was crucial in getting the project off the ground, contributing key ideas during an autumnal stroll down Fifth Avenue. Kim Crowley helped in many ways, especially in his constant search for stories. Thanks also to Joel and Dolly for feeding us stories from their local papers. Our reviewers were a goldmine of wonderful suggestions and comments:

Lubie Alatriste, New York, NY

Christel Antonellis, Boston, MA

Vicki Blaho, Los Angeles, CA

Susan Burke, Atlanta, GA

Gloria Horton, Pasadena, CA

Tay Lesley, Los Angeles, CA

Ellen Pentkowski, Chicago, IL

Barbara Jane Pers, Brooklyn, NY

Barbara Smith-Palinkas, Tampa, FL

Stephanie Snider, Suffolk County, NY

Candice Ramirez, Moreno Valley, CA

Christine Tierney, Houston, TX

Barbara Webster, Phoenix, AZ

Table of Contents

Engineer Is Enthusiastic About Odd New Home

Bruce Campbell cleaning his new home.

1. Quick Reading

Look at the pictures on page 3.
What is the story about?

Now read quickly to get the main idea.

PORTLAND, OR, USA [1]Bruce Campbell recently bought his dream home. Campbell, 49, is not someone who **follows the crowd. Instead of** a traditional house in the suburbs, he got a 727! [2]He **paid** $100,000 **for** his new home, which used to **belong to** the Greek airline Olympic Airways.

[3]Campbell's unusual home is parked on his rural property near the city of Portland. [4]He cleaned the cabin and **took out** most of the seats. "Now it's a palace in here!" he says. [5]The cabin *is* huge, but the bathrooms, **on the other hand,** are tiny. [6]Campbell **plans on** using the cockpit as his office.

[7]Campbell, an engineer, **is enthusiastic about** his new home. The plane is much stronger than most homes, he **points out**. And the roof will never leak!

[8]**At present,** Mr. Campbell is a bachelor. But **what if** he meets his **soul mate?** Then, he jokes, he'll buy a huge 747!

727: a large jet airplane made by Boeing
rural: in the countryside
cockpit: the place where the pilot sits to fly the plane

New idioms and expressions

be enthusiastic about something	like something very much
follow the crowd	do what everyone else does
instead of (doing) something	in the place of (doing) something
pay for something*	give money for something
belong to someone*	be the property of someone
take something out*	remove something
on the other hand	however; in contrast
plan on (doing) something*	expect (to do) something in the future
point something out*	explain something; show something
at present	now
what if	what will happen if
soul mate	perfect life partner

Words in parentheses ( ) can occur with an idiom, but don't have to.   *phrasal verb (see Lexicon, pp.116–150 and Appendix D, pp.111–115)

2. Listen

Cover the story and look only at these pictures. Listen to the story two or three times.

Note: As the tape or your teacher says a number, look at the corresponding picture.

3. Read the Story

Now read the story carefully. Pay special attention to the idioms so that you're ready for Exercise 4.

4. Listen and Complete

Close your book. Listen to the story again. When the tape or your teacher pauses, try to complete the idiom.

5. Match

Complete the idioms using the words in the box. Then write the number of the matching definition.

of	mate	the crowd	present
hand	out	about	

___5___ *a.* on the other _____*hand*_____   1. do what everyone else does

_____ *b.* at _____   2. remove

_____ *c.* follow _____   3. like very much

_____ *d.* instead _____   4. perfect life partner

_____ *e.* be enthusiastic _____   5. however

_____ *f.* take _____   6. in the place of

_____ *g.* soul _____   7. now

6. Tell the Story

Look only at the pictures and the New Idioms box on page 3. Tell the story using as many idioms as you can.

a. First, work with the whole class to retell the story.

b. Then tell the story to a partner or small group.

7. Answer the Questions

About the story. . . . .

a. How much did Campbell pay for his new home?

b. Who did the plane belong to before Campbell bought it?

c. What did he do to the cabin?

d. What does he plan on doing with the cockpit?

e. Why is Campbell enthusiastic about his new home?

f. What is his marital status at present?

g. What if he meets his soul mate?

h. Do you think Campbell will easily find a soul mate? Why or why not?

i. Would you be enthusiastic about living in a plane? Why or why not?

About you . . . .

j. What are you enthusiastic about?

k. Do you like to follow the crowd? (In fashion? In music?)

l. What kind of person would be a soul mate for you?

m. What things do you have to pay for every month?

n. Where are you living at present?

o. What do you plan on doing this weekend?

8. Take a Dictation

Listen to the tape or your teacher and write the dictation in your notebook.

9. Complete the Idioms

a. Sam certainly does not follow _____ *the crowd* _____ in fashion. At _____, his favorite outfit is a tuxedo jacket with shorts. He wears it every day.

b. Mira is enthusiastic _____ her studies and plans _____ becoming a judge.

c. Luka decided to pay _____ dinner with cash instead _____ with a credit card.

10. Look at Grammar

be enthusiastic about something
be enthusiastic about doing something
Henry's enthusiastic about soccer.
He's enthusiastic about playing soccer.

pay for something
pay money for something
I paid for dinner last night.
I paid $50 for dinner last night.

Note: You *pay* rent, *pay* bills, and *pay* tuition; but you *pay for* dinner, clothes, a car, and most other things.

take out something (**from** a place)
take something **out** (**of** a place)
I often take out books from the library.
I often take books out of the library.

Note: *Take out* is a transitive, separable phrasal verb. For further explanation on phrasal verbs, see Appendix D, pp. 111–115.

Complete the sentences with help from the grammar box above. Make sure they are true for you.

a. I paid _____ food last week.

b. I also paid for _____ last week.

c. Yesterday, I paid _____

   _____ .

d. I'm very enthusiastic _____

   because _____ .

e. I like to take _____ of the library.

11. Write a Dialogue

Work with a partner. Write a dialogue using at least four idioms from the unit. Act it out for the class.

12. Complete the Story

a. Fill in the blanks in this true story with idioms from the box. Put the verbs in the correct form and tense.

- **on the other hand**
- **point out** (v)
- **what if**
- **instead of**
- **plan on** (v)
- **be enthusiastic about** (v)
- **pay...for** (v)

Tired of Waste

Carlton, WA, USA Doug and Michelle Wilcox's dream house is good to the environment. The couple built their home from recycled materials (1) _____*instead of*_____ wood or brick. They used 1,600 old tires and thousands of tin cans. "There are six billion people on our planet, and we can't **keep on*** wasting precious natural resources," Doug Wilcox (2) _____.

The walls are made of old tires packed with dirt. Tin cans fill the walls between the tires. There are large windows on the south side of the house, which **take advantage of**** the sun to generate electricity.

The Wilcoxes built the house themselves. It was very hard work, but they (3) _____ only $20 a square foot _____ it. Traditional houses, (4) _____, cost between $45 and $65 a square foot.

(5) _____ there is an earthquake? Tom Griepentrog, a civil engineer, says, "The house is earthquake-proof. It's extremely safe and stable."

The Wilcoxes (6) _____ their tire house. "For us it feels right," says Michelle. In the future, they (7) _____ helping other people to build tire houses. "We want to teach people to respect the Earth," they say.

*keep on doing something: continue to do something

**take advantage of something: use something well

b. Read or tell the story to a partner.

Man Eats Out and Gets More Than He Ordered

1. Quick Reading

Look at the pictures on page 9.
What is the story about?

Now read quickly to get the main idea.

DELTONA, FL, USA ¹Henry Snowden, 31, decided to **eat out** one Friday night. He **pulled into** a drive-up window at Burger King. **Hungry as a bear**, he ordered a large burger, large fries, and a king-size drink. ²Snowden got his fast food **as well as** a big surprise. Stuffed inside one of the paper bags was $4,170!

³"I **looked at** the money as I ate. I knew immediately I should **give** it **back**," Snowden said. ⁴But Snowden did not return the money **right off the bat**. He went home to **sleep on it**. "I've got to say I was tempted to keep it," he admitted.

⁵Snowden **went back to** Burger King the next day to give back the money. ⁶Restaurant workers greeted him with tears in their eyes and gave him lunch **on the house**. ⁷They explained that the restaurant puts its bank deposits in paper bags to prevent robberies. **By mistake**, a clerk gave Snowden the wrong paper bag.

⁸Burger King may offer Snowden a reward. But Snowden says there's something even better—he **has a clear conscience**. "I'm glad I did the right thing. I feel better than I've ever felt."

---

be tempted: be strongly attracted to an idea

New idioms and expressions

eat out*	eat in a restaurant
pull into a place*	arrive at a place by car, bus, or train
(as) hungry as a bear	very hungry
as well as	and also
look at someone or something*	direct your eyes to someone or something
give something back (to someone)*	return something (to someone)
right off the bat	immediately
sleep on it	decide later, often the next day
have got to do something	have to do something; must do something
go back (to a place)*	return (to a place)
on the house	free; paid for by the merchant
by mistake	accidentally; in error
have a clear conscience	be free of guilt

*phrasal verb (see Lexicon and Appendix D)

2. Listen

Cover the story and look only at these pictures. Listen to the story two or three times.

3. Read the Story

Now read the story carefully. Pay special attention to the idioms so that you're ready for Exercise 4.

4. Listen and Complete

Close your book. Listen to the story again. When the tape or your teacher pauses, try to complete the idiom.

5. Match

Complete the idioms using the words in the box. Then write the number of the matching definition.

house	back	mistake	well as
a bear	out	the bat	

_____ *a.* as hungry as _____   **1.** eat in a restaurant

_____ *b.* right off _____   **2.** return something

_____ *c.* by _____   **3.** very hungry

_____ *d.* on the _____   **4.** immediately

_____ *e.* eat _____   **5.** and also

_____ *f.* as _____   **6.** accidentally

_____ *g.* give _____   **7.** free

6. Tell the Story

Look only at the pictures and the New Idioms box on page 9. Tell the story using as many idioms as you can.

a. First, work with the whole class to retell the story.

b. Then tell the story to a partner or small group.

7. Answer the Questions

About the story...

a. Why did Snowden decide to eat out?

b. Did he go inside the restaurant?

c. What did he get from the clerk?

d. What did he do as he ate?

e. Why didn't he return the money right off the bat?

f. When did he go back?

g. How did the workers thank him?

h. How does Snowden feel now?

i. What do you think of Snowden? Is he a good person? What would you do if you were *in his shoes* (in his situation)?

About you...

j. What do you like to eat when you're as hungry as a bear?

k. Do you like to eat out? Where?

l. Tell about something you did by mistake.

m. How important is it to have a clear conscience?

8. Take a Dictation

Listen to the tape or your teacher and write the dictation in your notebook.

9. Complete the Idioms

a. Gianni is hungry as _____. But he has no food at home, so he has to eat _____.

b. Mr. and Mrs. Ward always _____ back to the same restaurant, so sometimes they get their dessert and coffee on the _____.

c. The bank gave Sara too much money by _____. Sara is not sure whether to give it _____. She decided to sleep _____.

10. Look at Grammar

have got to do something

> *This weekend I've got to study. Bob's got to study too.*

Note: *have got to = have to = must*
> *Had to* is the past of all three expressions, and *will have to* is the future of all these.

give back something (**to** someone)
give something **back** (**to** someone)

> *I gave back the books to Giselle.*
> *I gave the books back to Giselle.*
> *I gave them back to her.*

Note: *Give back* is a phrasal verb. It is transitive and separable. See Appendix D for more information on phrasal verbs.

go back
go back to a place

> *Javier didn't like the weather in Alaska, and he'll never go back.*
> *Do you want to go back to that great store?*

Note: *Go back* and *go back to* are phrasal verbs. *Go back* is intransitive and inseparable. *Go back to* is transitive and inseparable. See Appendix D for more information. (An exception is *go back home*.)

Complete the sentences with help from the grammar box above. Make sure they are true for you.

a. I've got to _____ because

_____ .

b. _____ borrowed my _____ .

He(She) gave/didn't give _____ to me.

c. I want to go back _____

because _____ .

d. I visited _____ but didn't like it.

I don't want to ever _____ .

11. Write a Dialogue

Work with a partner. Write a dialogue using at least four idioms from the unit.
Act it out for the class.

12. Complete the Story

a. Fill in the blanks in this true story with idioms from the box. Put the verbs in the correct form and tense.

- **look at** (v)
- **right off the bat**
- **as well as**
- **hungry as a bear**
- **give back** (v)
- **go back** (v)
- **have a clear conscience** (v)

After 55 Years, Man Gives Back Stolen Ham

Tilly-la-Campagne, France It was July, 1944. The world was at war. Allied soldiers had just landed on the beaches of Normandy. The German army was leaving France.

Hans Kupperfahrenberg, 20, was a soldier in the German army in France. He had not eaten for several days and was (1) _____.
He stopped at a farmhouse in the tiny village of Tilly-la-Campagne. A French farmer, Louise Marie, made him some eggs. While she cooked, Hans hungrily (2) _____ a large ham in the fireplace. On his way out of the house, he stole the ham.

As the years **went by**,* Hans often **thought about**** what he had done. He felt guilty. How could he steal from a generous French woman? He wanted to apologize to Louise Marie, (3) _____ the ham, and (4) _____. But he didn't do it (5) _____. It took him a long time—55 years to be exact. Finally, in 1999, Hans (6) _____ to Tilly-la-Campagne. He presented two large hams—a French ham (7) _____ a German one—to Louise Marie, now 87.

"I was so hungry," Hans told Louise Marie at a ceremony in the Tilly town hall. "It was war. But it was wrong to eat your ham."

*go by: pass
**think about something: consider something

b. Read or tell the story to a partner.

Out On a Limb

1. Quick Reading

Look at the pictures on page 15.
What is the story about?

Now read quickly to get the main idea.

SAN FRANCISCO, CA, USA [1]Julia Butterfly, 24, has **gone out on a limb** for her beliefs. She has **spent two years** living in a giant redwood tree in Northern California, 180 feet above the ground. "I'm trying to save this tree," she says.

[2]Butterfly is a member of Earth First!, an environmental protection group. She and her group are **going head to head with** a lumber company, which owns the forest. [3]The company wants to **chop down** the 1000-year-old trees and sell the wood. [4]To protect the tree, Butterfly stays in it **around the clock**. Only 3% of redwood forests remain, **according to** Butterfly. "The world needs to know that the magnificent redwood forests are almost gone. I'm **taking a stand** for life in its beautiful form."

[5]Butterfly **puts up with** horrible weather. Powerful storms often hit her tree house. [6]She pulls up all her food with a rope. She cannot bathe. [7]Her only convenience is a cell phone to **keep in touch with** her family.

[8]Butterfly plans to stay in the tree as long as she can. What does she **look forward to** back in civilization? "I'd like to **take a** hot **shower**," she says.

New idioms and expressions

go out on a limb	do something that could have dangerous consequences
spend time doing something	use time to do something
go head to head (with someone)	argue or fight (with someone)
chop something down*	cut something down, usually a tree
around the clock	continuously; without a break
according to someone or something	as said by someone or something
take a stand	clearly and loudly declare your point of view
put up with someone or something*	endure or tolerate someone or something
keep in touch (with someone)	communicate regularly (with someone)
look forward to (doing) something*	anticipate (doing) something with pleasure
take a shower or bath	wash yourself in the shower or bath

*phrasal verb (see Lexicon and Appendix D)

🔲 2. Listen

Cover the story and look only at these pictures. Listen to the story two or three times.

3. Read the Story

Now read the story carefully. Pay special attention to the idioms so that you're ready for Exercise 4.

4. Listen and Complete

Close your book. Listen to the story again. When the tape or your teacher pauses, try to complete the idiom.

5. Match

Complete the idioms using the words in the box. Then write the number of the matching definition.

| stand | clock | up with | forward to |
| touch with | to head with | | down |

_____ **a.** keep in _____   1. continuously

_____ **b.** around the _____   2. tolerate

_____ **c.** chop _____   3. clearly declare your point of view

_____ **d.** go head _____   4. fight with

_____ **e.** put _____   5. communicate regularly with

_____ **f.** take a _____   6. anticipate with pleasure

_____ **g.** look _____   7. cut down

6. Tell the Story

Look only at the pictures and the New Idioms box on page 15. Tell the story using as many idioms as you can.
a. First, work with the whole class to retell the story.
b. Then tell the story to a partner or small group.

7. Answer the Questions

About the story . . . .

a. Why is Butterfly in the tree?

b. How much time has she spent living there?

c. What is Earth First!? Why is it going head to head with a lumber company?

d. According to Butterfly, why is it important to take a stand?

e. What problems does she have to put up with in the tree house?

f. Why does she need a cell phone?

g. What does Butterfly look forward to?

h. Do you think Butterfly has the right to stay in the tree? Why or why not?

About you . . . .

i. Which social or political causes are important to you? Which one(s) would you go out on a limb for?

j. Do you care about the environment? Tell how you help save the earth.

k. Are there environmental groups in your country? What are their goals?

l. Tell about a time when you put up with an inconvenience such as horrible weather or no electrical power.

m. Imagine that you were living in a tree for a year. What would be difficult to put up with? What would you look forward to? What would you spend time doing?

8. Take a Dictation

Listen to the tape or your teacher and write the dictation in your notebook.

9. Complete the Idioms

a. Alma's working around _____ on her new novel. She _____ all her time writing.

b. Fathi has put _____ cold weather for four months and is looking _____ summer.

c. George is always fighting with his wife. Now he's going _____ with her about which TV show to watch.

10. Look at Grammar

> **look forward to** something
> **look forward to doing** something
> *I'm looking forward to dinner.*
> *I'm looking forward to having dinner with you.*
>
> **Note:** This phrasal verb is often used in the present continuous. It is also used in the simple present when addressing someone directly, as in *I look forward to seeing you again* or, in a letter, *I look forward to hearing from you.*
>
> **keep/stay in touch**
> **keep/stay in touch with** someone
> *Good-bye, Joe. Stay in touch!*
> *She keeps in touch with old friends by e-mail.*
>
> **Note:** The imperative *Keep in touch!* is a standard parting for friends who don't see each other very often. *Stay in touch* means the same thing. Compare with the expressions *get in touch with* (=contact someone) and *lose touch with* (=lose contact with).
> *It's very hard to get in touch with Silvia. She's never home!*
> *I've lost touch with Toshi. He moved and didn't leave his new number.*
>
> **put up with** someone
> **put up with** something
> *I cannot put up with nasty people.*
> *I cannot put up with nastiness.*
>
> **according to** someone
> **according to** something (a source of information)
> *According to my mother, I am very stubborn.*
> *According to today's newspaper, women work harder than men.*
>
> **Note:** Do not use *me* after *according to.* Instead, say *in my opinion.*

Complete the sentences with help from the grammar box above. Make sure they are true for you.

a. I'm really looking forward _____

     because _____ .

b. I regularly keep in touch _____ .

c. It's hard for me to put up _____

     because _____ .

d. According _____ , I am _____

     _____ .

e. In my opinion, _____ .

11. Write a Dialogue

Work with a partner. Write a dialogue using at least four idioms from the unit.
Act it out for the class.

12. Complete the Dialogue

a. Two university students are talking about a street demonstration to protest higher tuition costs. Fill in the blanks with an idiom from the box. Put the verbs in the correct form and tense.

> - **around the clock**
> - **go head to head with** (v)
> - **put up with** (v)
> - **keep in touch** (v)
> - **go out on a limb** (v)
> - **according to**

Hey, Mira. I heard about the protest march on Saturday. **Way to go***!

Yeah, we're really (1) _____ the university administration. I've been working (2) _____ on it.

You're brave, girl, to organize this thing. You're really (3) _____.

Yeah, well...

(4) _____ my brother, the university president is not too happy about it.

Yeah, I know. But we can't (5) _____ that huge tuition increase. It's not fair

That's for sure. Well, **I've got to run****. Good luck on Saturday.

Thanks, so long! (6) _____!

---

* Way to go!: Good work! (informal)

** have got to run: must leave quickly

b. Work with a partner. Role-play the dialogue together.

On Top of the World

4

Climbing Mount Everest.

1. **Quick Reading**

Look at the pictures on page 21.
What is the story about?

Now read quickly to get the main idea.

KATMANDU, NEPAL **1**As a boy in Wales, Tom Whittaker **had his heart set on** climbing mountains. He moved to the U.S. and became a skilled climber.

2In 1979, a drunk driver hit his car. Whittaker, then age 30, lost his right foot. This was **a bitter pill to swallow**. **3**However, he refused to **give up** climbing. Instead, he decided to **break new ground** as a disabled person. He **set his sights on** Mount Everest, the tallest mountain in the world. It's also the most dangerous; one in six climbers dies there.

4Year in and year out for more than ten years, Whittaker trained hard for his dream. **5**With the help of doctors and engineers, he designed a strong artificial foot to climb the terrible mountain. **6**In 1989, Whittaker **made a first attempt to** climb, but bad weather **forced** him **back**. In 1995, he made a second attempt. This time, illness forced him back.

7Finally, in 1998, Whittaker reached the roof of the world. "I arrived just as the sun **came up**," he said. He **was on top of the world**! **8**Whittaker **made history** as the first disabled person to climb Mount Everest.

New idioms and expressions

be on top of the world · · · · · · · · · · · · · · · ·	be very happy
have one's heart set on something · · · · ·	want something very much
a bitter pill to swallow · · · · · · · · · · · · · ·	a difficult thing to accept
give up (doing) something* · · · · · · · · · · ·	stop or quit (doing) something
break new ground · · · · · · · · · · · · · · · · · ·	do something that has not been done before
set one's sights on (doing) something · · ·	choose (to do) something as a goal
year in and year out · · · · · · · · · · · · · · ·	continuously for many years
make an attempt (to do something) · · · · ·	try (to do something)
force someone back* · · · · · · · · · · · · · · · ·	make someone go back
come up* ·	rise (referring to the sun, moon, etc.)
make history ·	do something that will be remembered in history books

*phrasal verb (see Lexicon and Appendix D)

2. Listen

Cover the story and look only at these pictures. Listen to the story two or three times.

3. Read the Story

Now read the story carefully. Pay special attention to the idioms so that you're ready for Exercise 4.

4. Listen and Complete

Close your book. Listen to the story again. When the tape or your teacher pauses, try to complete the idiom.

5. Match

Complete the idioms using the words in the box. Then write the number of the matching definition.

of the world	set on	attempt	ground
out	history	to swallow	

____ *a.* make an _____   1. be very happy

____ *b.* be on top _____   2. want very much

____ *c.* break new _____   3. do something no one has done before

____ *d.* have one's heart _____   4. try

____ *e.* a bitter pill _____   5. continuously for many years

____ *f.* year in and year _____   6. do something that will be remembered

____ *g.* make _____   7. a difficult thing to accept

6. Tell the Story

Look only at the pictures and the New Idioms box on page 21. Tell the story using as many idioms as you can.
a. First, work with the whole class to retell the story.
b. Then tell the story to a partner or small group.

7. Answer the Questions

About the story...

a. As a boy, what did Whittaker have his heart set on?

b. How did he feel when he had the accident?

c. After the accident, what did Whittaker set his sights on?

d. What did he do year in and year out?

e. What happened when he made a first attempt at Everest? What happened the second time?

f. Why did Whittaker decide to climb such a difficult mountain?

g. When did he arrive on the roof of the world? How did he feel?

h. Why has he made history?

i. What do you think of Whittaker?

About you...

j. Who do you admire who has broken new ground or made history?

k. What are you setting your sights on for the future?

l. Would you like to make history? If so, for what?

8. Take a Dictation

Listen to the tape or your teacher and write the dictation in your notebook.

9. Complete the Idioms

a. Jorge made an _____ to ice skate, but after falling so much, he decided to give it _____.

b. Hyunwoo has her sights _____ becoming a doctor. She has studied year in and _____ for ten years.

c. Einstein _____ history when he broke new _____ in physics.

d. Francoise had to give _____ skiing when she broke her leg. It was a bitter _____.

10. Look at Grammar

make an attempt
make an attempt at something
make an attempt at doing something
make an attempt to do something
  It's hard for Lydia to learn Japanese, but she's making an attempt.
  Lydia is making an attempt at Japanese.
  Lydia is making an attempt at learning Japanese.
  Lydia is making an attempt to learn Japanese.

break new ground
break new ground in something
break new ground by doing something
break new ground when...
  Picasso broke new ground.
  Picasso broke new ground in the art of painting.
  He broke new ground by painting in a new style.
  He broke new ground when he started painting in a Cubist style.

have one's heart set on something
have one's heart set on doing something
  June had her heart set on a trip to Greece.
  She had her heart set on going to Greece.

set one's sights on something
set one's sights on doing something
  She is setting her sights on a medical degree.
  She is setting her sights on becoming a doctor.

Complete the sentences with help from the grammar box above. Make sure they are true for you.

a. I admire _____ because he/she broke new

   ground _____.

b. It's difficult, but I am making an attempt to _____.

c. I made my first attempt at _____

   in (date, place) _____.

d. I have my heart set _____

   before the end of the year.

e. I have set my sights _____,

   so I must _____.

11. Write a Dialogue

Work with a partner. Write a dialogue using at least four idioms from the unit.
Act it out for the class.

12. Complete the Dialogue

a. Two friends, Tonya and Miguel, are talking about Tonya's restaurant business. Fill in the blanks with idioms from the box. Put the verbs in the correct form and tense.

> - **break new ground** (v)
> - **year in and year out**
> - **on top of the world**
> - **make an attempt** (v)
> - **have one's heart set on** (v)
> - **give up** (v)

Hi, Tonya. It's Miguel. I got your message. How are you?

Not exactly
(1) _____ .

What's the matter?

Bad news. My restaurant is losing money. Business is bad. I might have to close it.

(2) _____ the restaurant? You can't do that!

Well, I (3) _____ making it a success, as you know. But what can I do? I saved my money (4) _____ to start the place. Now the money's almost gone! I**'m broke*!**

Well, you sure
(5) _____ with your fabulous cooking.

Thanks, but...

Listen, what about advertising? The problem is no one knows about your place. (6) _____ to better inform people.

OK. One last try. Will you help me design an ad?

*be broke: have no money (informal)

b. Work with a partner. Role-play the dialogue together.

Boy Fights Lion Tooth and Nail

1. Quick Reading

Look at the pictures on page 27.
What is the story about?

Now read quickly to get the main idea.

MISSOULA, MT, USA   **1**On a fine summer day, Aaron Hall, 16, **set out on** a hike in the mountains of Montana with a group of young children. As a camp counselor, Hall **was in charge of** the children's safety.

2Hall was walking **in front of** six-year-old Dante Swallow when he heard Dante scream. **3**He turned around and **got the shock of his life**. An animal had Dante by the neck and was dragging him away. **At first glance** the animal **looked like** a dog, but then Hall saw the face of a mountain lion. **4**He reacted **in a flash**. He began kicking and hitting the lion. He **fought tooth and nail.**

5The lion **let go of** Dante and **backed off**, running into the bushes. **6**Hall gave Dante first aid. Then he jumped into a nearby truck and drove the boy down the mountain. **7**At the hospital Dante got stitches in his neck. What **a close call**! The lion's teeth had just missed Dante's main artery.

8"I **was** really **scared of** that lion," Hall said afterwards. "I don't even remember fighting him." He is now a hero in his community. "What he did is just incredible," said Dante's grateful parents.

---

artery: a tube that carries fresh blood from the heart through the body

New idioms and expressions

fight tooth and nail · · · · · · · · · · · · · · · · ·	fight very hard
set out (on a hike, a walk, a trip)* · · · · ·	begin (a hike, a walk, a trip, an adventure, etc.)
be in charge (of someone or something)	be responsible (for someone or something)
in front of someone or something · · · · ·	ahead of; before someone or something
get the shock of one's life · · · · · · · · · · ·	be extremely surprised and scared
at first glance ·	at the first quick look
look like someone or something · · · · · ·	be similar in appearance to someone or something
in a flash ·	very quickly
let go (of someone or something)* · · · ·	release (someone or something)
back off (from someone)* · · · · · · · · · · ·	move in reverse; stop threatening (someone)
a close call ·	a narrow escape
be scared of someone or something · · · ·	fear; be afraid of someone or something

*phrasal verb (see Lexicon and Appendix D)

 2. Listen

Cover the story and look only at these pictures. Listen to the story two or three times.

3. Read the Story

Now read the story carefully. Pay special attention to the idioms so that you're ready for Exercise 4.

4. Listen and Complete

Close your book. Listen to the story again. When the tape or your teacher pauses, try to complete the idiom.

5. Match

Complete the idioms using the words in the box. Then write the number of the matching definition.

charge of	flash	glance	call
tooth and nail	off	of one's life	

____ a. get the shock _____   1. a narrow escape

____ b. back _____   2. very quickly

____ c. a close _____   3. be responsible for

____ d. fight _____   4. at the first quick look

____ e. be in _____   5. be very surprised and scared

____ f. at first _____   6. move in reverse

____ g. in a _____   7. fight hard

6. Tell the Story

Look only at the pictures and the New Idioms box on page 27. Tell the story using as many idioms as you can.
a. First, work with the whole class to retell the story.
b. Then tell the story to a partner or small group.

7. Answer the Questions

About the story . . . .

a. What was Hall in charge of?

b. What did the animal look like at first glance?

c. How did Hall react when he saw it was a lion? How would you react in the same situation?

d. What did the lion do after Hall fought him tooth and nail?

e. Why did Dante have a close call?

f. What is your opinion of Hall?

About you . . . .

g. Tell about a time when you got the shock of your life.

h. Are you scared of any animals? Which ones?

i. Tell about a close call you have had in your life. What happened?

j. Do you like to be in charge of things? Explain.

8. Take a Dictation

Listen to the tape or your teacher and write the dictation in your notebook.

9. Complete the Idioms

a. The dog and cat fought _____. Finally the dog let _____ the cat and backed _____ .

b. The accident happened _____ flash. The cyclist was not injured, but it was a close _____ .

c. The woman got the shock _____ when she opened the cabin door and saw a bear _____ of her.

10. Look at Grammar

> **be scared of** someone
> **be scared of** something
> **be scared of doing** something
> > *The child is scared of his neighbor.*
> > *The child is scared of the dark.*
> > *The child is scared of sleeping in the dark.*
> **Note:** *be scared of = be afraid of = be frightened of*
>
> **be in charge of** someone
> **be in charge of** something
> **be in charge of doing** something
> > *Esperanza is in charge of the children.*
> > *Esperanza is in charge of the party.*
> > *Esperanza is in charge of cooking and cleaning.*
>
> X **looks like** Y
> X **and** Y **look alike**
> > *Jill looks like her mother.*
> > *Jill and her mother look alike.*
> **Note:** You can also use *look like* in the following ways:
> > *They look like they're cold. (= They appear to be cold.)*
> > *It looks like rain. (= It is probably going to rain.)*
> > *It looks like Jose is going to stay. (= Jose is probably going to stay.)*

Complete the sentences with help from the grammar box above. Make sure they are true for you.

a. As a child, I was scared _____.

    Now I'm scared _____.

b. Growing up in my family, I was in charge _____,

    and my _____ was in charge _____.

c. I look _____.

d. My _____ and I look/don't look _____.

11. Write a Dialogue

Work with a partner. Write a dialogue using at least four idioms from the unit.
Act it out for the class.

12. Complete the Story

a. Fill in the blanks in this true story with idioms from the box. Put the verbs in the correct form and tense.

- be scared of (v)
- in front of
- set out (v)
- back off (v)
- get the shock of one's life (v)
- a close call
- in a flash
- in charge of

Senator Has a Close Call

Whitefish, Mt, USA For many years Senator Bob Brown worked in the Montana Legislature, where he was (1)_____ making new laws for the state. But Brown **is retired*** now and spends much of his time outdoors.

One recent summer day Brown (2) _____ with his dog Mishka to do some fishing. On his way to the river, he (3) _____ . Mishka came out from some bushes and behind her was a grizzly bear! (4) _____ , Brown climbed a dead pine tree which had no branches. "I went up that tree as fast as I could go. If you don't think a fat guy can climb a tree, think again," he said. The bear stood (5) _____ Brown and tried to grab his feet. "I (6) _____ falling. I was so tired. I knew I couldn't stay up in the tree much longer." Mishka, meanwhile, was hiding quietly in the bushes.

Luckily, the bear eventually got bored and (7) _____ . Brown and Mishka escaped in the other direction. It was (8) _____ !

* be retired: be no longer working

b. Read or tell the story to a partner.

Face-to-Face after 56 Years

6

1. Quick Reading

Look at the pictures on page 33.
What is the story about?

Now read quickly to get the main idea.

ST PETERSBURG, RUSSIA ¹In 1941, the Nazis entered Russia. Anna Babken, 17, **was pregnant** and living in Luzhsky, near St. Petersburg. ²The Nazis destroyed her town and **burned down** her house, so she **gave birth to** her daughter, Ludmilla, outdoors in a field.

³In 1942, the Nazis took Anna to a labor camp in Germany. She lost Ludmilla. "I don't know who took my daughter from my arms," she says.

⁴Anna **lived through** the war. Afterwards, she **searched for** Ludmilla, but couldn't find her. ⁵She emigrated to the U.S. and had two more children. But she couldn't stop **thinking about** Ludmilla. Was she alive? Where was she? Anna always put an empty chair at the dinner table for her lost daughter.

⁶**Year after year,** Anna wrote letters to the Soviet government. Finally, in 1963, she **found out** that Ludmilla was alive and living in Russia. They started writing, but there were restrictions against travel into or out of the Soviet Union. As a result, they couldn't **get together**.

⁷When the Soviet Union collapsed in 1989, they began to **make plans for** a reunion. ⁸Finally, in 1998, after 56 years, Anna and Ludmilla met **face-to-face** in Boston. It was **a dream come true**. "I knew someday I would find her," says Anna, now 74. "Now my empty chair is filled."

restrictions: limitations on one's freedom

Mother and daughter together, Anna Arabian (left) and Ludmilla Ulyanova (right).

New idioms and expressions

face-to-face	in direct contact; in person
be pregnant	be going to have a baby
burn something down*	destroy something by fire
give birth (to a baby)	have a baby
live through something*	survive something
search for someone or something*	look everywhere for someone or something
think about someone or something*	remember; consider someone or something
year after year	regularly for many years
find something out*	learn or discover something
get together (with someone)	meet and spend time with someone
make plans for something	plan to do something
a dream come true	a dream that has become a reality

*phrasal verb (see Lexicon and Appendix D)

2. Listen

Cover the story and look only at these pictures. Listen to the story two or three times.

3. Read the Story

Now read the story carefully. Pay special attention to the idioms so that you're ready for Exercise 4.

4. Listen and Complete

Close your book. Listen to the story again. When the tape or your teacher pauses, try to complete the idiom.

5. Match

Complete the idioms using the words in the box. Then write the number of the matching definition.

down	come true	out	pregnant
	after year	through	birth to

____ *a.* give _____   1. learn or discover

____ *b.* burn _____   2. survive

____ *c.* year _____   3. have a baby

____ *d.* a dream _____   4. destroy by fire

____ *e.* live _____   5. be going to have a baby

____ *f.* find _____   6. a dream that becomes a reality

____ *g.* be _____   7. regularly for many years

6. Tell the Story

Look only at the pictures and the New Idioms box on page 33. Tell the story using as many idioms as you can.
a. First, work with the whole class to retell the story.
b. Then tell the story to a partner or small group.

7. Answer the Questions

About the story. . . . .

a. Why did Anna give birth to her baby outdoors?

b. What happened to her in 1942?

c. What did Anna do right after the war? Was she successful?

d. After Anna came to the U.S., what couldn't she stop doing?

e. Who did she write to year after year?

f. What did Anna find out in 1963?

g. Why couldn't she and her daughter get together?

h. When did they finally meet face to face? How did they feel?

About you. . . . .

i. Where are there wars today? Why are the two sides fighting?

j. Do you know someone who lived through a war? Discuss.

k. Do you often think about someone far away? Will you get together in the future?

l. When and where did your mother give birth to you?

m. Anna waited 56 years for her dream to come true. Do you have a dream? When do you think it will come true?

n. Are you making plans for a trip? Tell the class.

8. Take a Dictation

Listen to the tape or your teacher and write the dictation in your notebook.

9. Complete the Idioms

a. When the three sisters got _____, they made _____ for their trip to Paris.

b. Isis gave _____ a beautiful baby boy. For her, it was a _____ come true. Now she's thinking _____ having another baby.

c. Seiko and I speak on the phone all the time, but we have never met face-_____.

10. Look at Grammar

get together
get together with someone
  Why don't we try to get together?
  I got together with Abdul last week.

Note: This expression is often followed by a time expression and *for*.
  Let's get together tomorrow for dinner.
  We'll get together soon for a drink.
  Can you get together with us tonight for a chat?
  She and I will get together next week for a cup of coffee.

give birth
give birth to someone
  Ida Simons gave birth last night.
  She gave birth to a healthy baby boy.

Note the difference between *give birth to* and *be born*:
  Anna gave birth to Ludmilla in 1941.
  Ludmilla was born in 1941.

make plans
make plans for something
make plans to do something
  I'm sorry, I can't come. I already made plans.
  I made plans for a trip to Montreal.
  I made plans to take a trip to Montreal.

Complete the sentences with help from the grammar box above. Make sure they are true for you.

a. My mother gave birth _____.

b. I _____ born _____.

c. I hope that _____ and I can get together soon for

   _____.

d. I got together _____

   for _____.

e. I'm making plans _____.

11. Write a Dialogue

Work with a partner. Write a dialogue using at least four idioms from the unit.
Act it out for the class.

12. Complete the Story

a. Fill in the blanks in this true story with idioms from the box. Put the verbs in the correct form and tense.

> - **face-to-face**
> - **think about (v)**
> - **year after year**
> - **give birth to (v)**
> - **search for (v)**
> - **a dream come true**
> - **find out (v)**

A Dream Come True

Beijing, China In 1928, a woman in Wuhan, China, (1) _____ twin girls, Zhou Qunying and Peng Meiying. The family was so poor that they had to give baby Zhou to an orphanage. Zhou was adopted by a vegetable farmer and his wife, who never told the child about her past.

According to the China Daily, young Peng (2) _____ her twin sister all the time. When she was older, Peng (3) _____ Zhou (4) _____, **to no avail.***

But in 1995, Peng's daughter saw an old woman selling tea in a city park in Wuhan. She noticed that the tea seller looked just like her mother!

Peng went to the park to see the tea seller. After 67 years, the two sisters met (5) _____. Peng and Zhou had a medical check and (6) _____ they had the same blood type. The probability of their being twins was 99.9999 percent. For Peng, it was (7) _____.

* to no avail: without success
recycled idioms: according to, look like

b. Read or tell the story to a partner.

Globe-Trotting Frog Comes Home

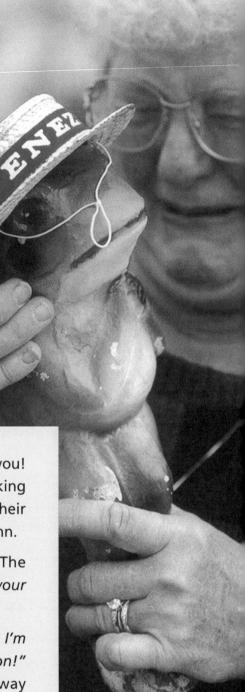

1. Quick Reading

Look at the pictures on page 39.
What is the story about?

Now read quickly to get the main idea.

Gertrude Knight sheds tears of joy at the return of her frog.

SWANSEA, MA, USA If you love a good mystery, this story is for you! **1**One spring day, Gertrude and John Knight, both 67, were working in their yard. They noticed that the ten-pound cement frog in their garden was gone. **2**"I thought some kids **ripped** it **off**," said John.

3But several weeks later, John began to **change his mind.** The Knights got a strange postcard that said, *"**I'm sick of** sitting in your garden. Had to **get away**. Love, the Frog."*

4Then the Knights got a letter from New York. *"Dear Ma and Pa, I'm in New York! I should **be back** by Christmas. I'll write again soon!"* Inside the letter was a photo of the frog at a New York subway station.

5For the next eight months, cards and pictures arrived from around the world. The Knights **heard from** the frog in Indonesia, Sweden, and Italy. **6**A letter from Paris said, *"Hi Mom and Dad, Can't stay here too long. They eat frog legs!"* Finally, the frog **dropped** them **a line** from Japan, which said *"**I'll catch you later,** around Christmas."*

7**Sure enough**, just before Christmas, the **globe-trotting** frog arrived home in a limousine. There was also champagne and a letter for the Knights. *"Thanks for **being good sports!**"* it said. **8**The Knights **don't have a clue** who took the frog. But they sure **got a kick out of** his adventure!

New idioms and expressions

globe-trotting ··········	traveling around the world
rip something off / rip someone off* ·······	steal something / steal from someone
change one's mind ················	change one's opinion or point of view
be sick of something ·············	be tired of; be bored with something
get away* ·················	leave one's daily routine; go on vacation
be back ·················	be again where you were before
hear from someone* ·········	receive a phone call, letter, or e-mail from someone
drop someone a line ···········	write a short letter to someone
I'll catch you later ············	I'll see you later
sure enough ················	as expected
be a good sport ···············	be able to laugh at jokes and pranks that involve you
not have a clue ··············	not know anything
get a kick out of something ··········	enjoy something a lot

*phrasal verb (see Lexicon and Appendix D)

🖭 2. Listen

Cover the story and look only at these pictures. Listen to the story two or three times.

3. Read the Story

Now read the story carefully. Pay special attention to the idioms so that you're ready for Exercise 4.

4. Listen and Complete

Close your book. Listen to the story again. When the tape or your teacher pauses, try to complete the idiom.

5. Match

Complete the idioms using the words in the box. Then write the number of the matching definition.

| enough | | sport | | from | | line |
| | mind | | out of | | off | |

____ a. change your _____   1. as expected

____ b. rip _____   2. enjoy a lot

____ c. get a kick _____   3. receive a letter or call from

____ d. drop a _____   4. steal

____ e. be a good _____   5. write a short letter

____ f. hear _____   6. be able to laugh at jokes about you

____ g. sure _____   7. change your opinion or point of view

6. Tell the Story

Look only at the pictures and the New Idioms box on page 39. Tell the story using as many idioms as you can.
a. First, work with the whole class to retell the story.
b. Then tell the story to a partner or small group.

7. Answer the Questions

About the story . . . .

a. What did John Knight think happened to the frog at first?

b. When and why did he change his mind?

c. According to the postcard, why did the frog have to get away?

d. When did he promise to be back?

e. For how long did the Knights continue to hear from the frog?

f. What did the card from Japan say?

g. When did the globe-trotting frog arrive home?

h. What was the message in the letter?

i. Do the Knights know who took the frog?

j. How did they feel about his adventure?

k. In your opinion, what kind of person took the frog?

About you . . . .

l. Do you like to get away? Where do you go?

m. How often do you drop your friends and family a line? How often do you hear from them?

n. What kinds of sports or adventures do you get a kick out of?

o. Are you a globe-trotter (or would you like to be)? Tell about your travels (or your plans).

8. Take a Dictation

Listen to the tape or your teacher and write the dictation in your notebook.

9. Complete the Idioms

a. Hector wanted to fix the sink, but he changed his
_____ . He realizes he doesn't have a
_____ how to do it.

b. Tina and Diego are a _____ couple. They
get _____ out of traveling the world.

c. A thief ripped _____ my bike.

10. Look at Grammar

be sick of something
be sick of doing something
> *Jose was sick of the hard work.*
> *Jose was sick of working so hard.*

Note: *be sick of = be tired of = be sick and tired of* (The third expression is stronger than the first two.)

get away
get away from something
> *Daisy is tired; she needs to get away.*
> *Daisy needs to get away from the stress of her job.*

Note: You can get away from *work, the stress, the routine, the city, it all* (= everything), and *the rat race* (= the fast pace of everyday life). *Get away* is intransitive; *get away from* is transitive and inseparable. For more information on phrasal verbs, see Appendix D.

rip off something / **rip** something **off**
rip off someone / **rip** someone **off**
> *That man ripped off my bag!/That man ripped my bag off!/That man ripped it off.*
> *Someone ripped off my mother./Someone ripped my mother off./Someone ripped her off.*

Note: *Rip off* is a transitive, separable phrasal verb. Remember that when you use a pronoun (*it, her,* etc.) with a separable phrasal verb, it must go between the verb and the particle. See Appendix D for more information on phrasal verbs.

Complete the sentences with help from the grammar box above. Make sure they are true for you.

a. I'm sick of _____

   because _____.

b. I'd like to get away _____

   because _____.

c. Someone ripped _____.

11. Write a Dialogue

Work with a partner. Write a dialogue using at least four idioms from the unit.
Act it out for the class.

12. Complete the Dialogue

a. A mother and her 18-year-old daughter, Lucy, are saying goodbye. Lucy **is about to*** move to San Francisco. Fill in the blanks with idioms from the box. Put the verbs in the correct form and tense.

be sick of (v)
be back (v)
not have a clue (v)
change one's mind (v)
get away (v)
drop a line (v)
catch you later (v)
hear from (v)

Lucy, there's still time to (1)_____ about this.

No, Mom. I've got to (2)_____. This town is too small for me. I (3)_____ it. San Francisco is calling me!

I know, honey. Don't forget to call and write. I'm afraid we'll never (4)_____ you.

Don't worry. I (5)_____ every week. And I (6)_____ here for Christmas vacation. That's only three months away!

Yeah, that's true. How long do you think it will take you to find a job?

I (7)_____, Mom. I'll just have to see. **I'd better**** go. Goodbye, Mom.

Goodbye, sweetheart. I'll miss you. Give me a big kiss. Drive carefully and call the minute you get there.

OK. Bye, Mom. (8)_____!

* be about to do something: be ready to do something

** had better: should

b. Work with a partner. Role-play the dialogue together.

Review 1 2 3 4 5 6 7 8 9 10 11 12 13 14

A. Fill in the bubbles: What are these people saying? Fill in each speech bubble with an appropriate sentence from the box at the bottom of the page.

1.

> I don't have a clue.

6.

2.

7.

3.

8.

4.

9.

5.

10.

Let go of me!	This is a bitter pill to swallow.
I don't have a clue.	I'm sick of this weather.
This is on the house.	I'm looking forward to getting away.
I'll catch you later!	We're breaking new ground.
This is a dream come true!	I'm hungry as a bear.

B. Odd one out: Cross out the word or phrase that does NOT go with the first word.

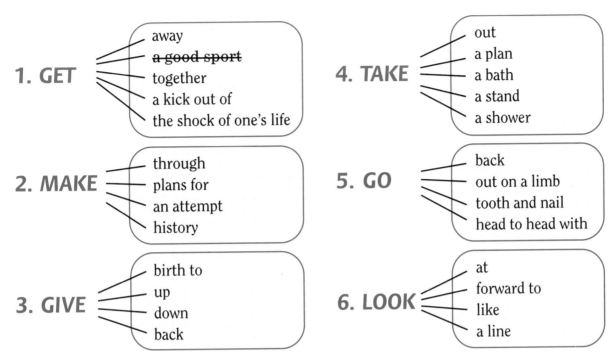

1. GET
- away
- ~~a good sport~~
- together
- a kick out of
- the shock of one's life

4. TAKE
- out
- a plan
- a bath
- a stand
- a shower

2. MAKE
- through
- plans for
- an attempt
- history

5. GO
- back
- out on a limb
- tooth and nail
- head to head with

3. GIVE
- birth to
- up
- down
- back

6. LOOK
- at
- forward to
- like
- a line

C. Idioms that use *out*: Match the idioms with their definitions.

_e_ 1. eat **out**

____ 2. find **out**

____ 3. go **out** on a limb

____ 4. point **out**

____ 5. take **out**

____ 6. year in and year **out**

____ 7. get a kick **out** of

a. discover

b. explain

c. remove

d. take a dangerous position

e. go to a restaurant

f. enjoy very much

g. regularly for a long time

D. *In or on?* Fill in the blanks of these idioms with *in* or *on*.

1. be ___*in*___ charge of

2. be _____ top of the world

3. have one's heart set _____

4. _____ a flash

5. _____ front of

6. _____ the house

7. keep _____ touch with

8. _____ the other hand

9. plan _____

10. set one's sights _____

11. sleep _____ it

12. year _____ and year out

E. Parts of the body: Many idioms use parts of the body. Finish these idioms and then match them to their definitions.

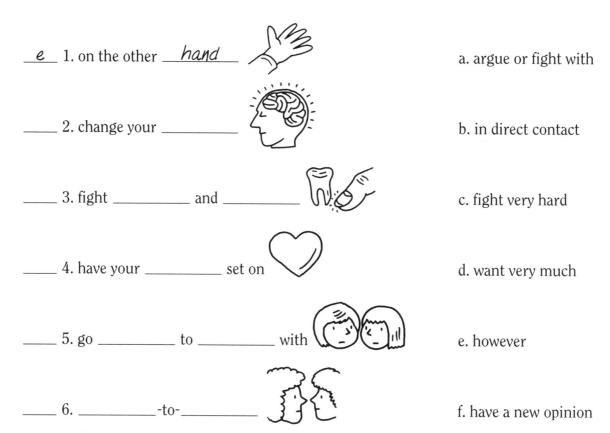

_e_ 1. on the other _hand_

_____ 2. change your _____

_____ 3. fight _____ and _____

_____ 4. have your _____ set on

_____ 5. go _____ to _____ with

_____ 6. _____-to-_____

a. argue or fight with

b. in direct contact

c. fight very hard

d. want very much

e. however

f. have a new opinion

F. Complete the sentences: Complete the sentences so they are true for you.

1. I should drop _____ a line.

2. I sometimes go head to head _____
   because _____.

3. Before the end of the week, I've got to _____.

4. I'm scared of _____.

5. I always get a kick out _____.

6. I often think about _____.

7. It's hard for me to put up _____.

8. I try to keep in touch _____.

9. I'm looking forward _____.

10. I recently heard from _____.

G. Good or bad? Is the speaker feeling good or bad? Write the sentences in the correct box.

I'm getting a kick out of this.
Will I live through this?
I have a clear conscience.
Someone ripped me off.
I can't put up with this anymore.
You're my soul mate.

We're fighting tooth and nail.
This is a bitter pill to swallow.
It's a dream come true!
I'm on top of the world.
I've really got to get away.

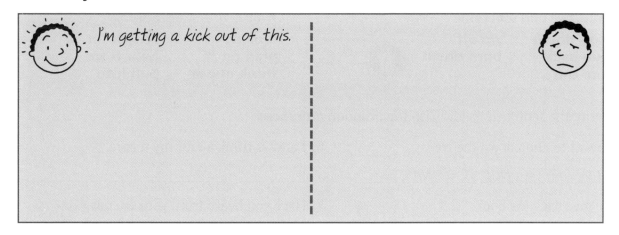

I'm getting a kick out of this.

H. Idioms in pictures: Use the pictures to complete the idioms.

1. I'm as hungry as a ____*bear*____ ! How about you?

2. I didn't expect that to happen! I got the _____ of my life.

3. We don't see him much. He seems to work around the _____ .

4. He's not very original. He always follows the _____ .

5. I'm scared of what could happen. They have really gone out on a _____ .

6. When I get to work, I read my e-mail right off the _____ .

I. Phrasal verbs: Review the lists of phrasal verbs below.

Transitive *and separable*		Transitive *and inseparable*	
chop down	rip off	look at	search for
give back	burn down	plan on	hear from
take out		think about	pull into

Now rewrite the sentences below with the pronoun *it* or *them*.

1. They want to chop down the tree.

   They want to chop it down. .

2. Please give back my book.

   _____.

3. I'm searching for my glasses.

   _____.

4. I didn't look at the photos.

   _____.

5. Someone ripped off my wallet.

   _____.

6. I always think about my future.

   _____.

7. Have you heard from your friends yet?

   _____.

8. Let's take out the bikes.

   _____.

9. She was careless and burned down the cabin.

   _____.

10. Pull into the parking space slowly.

   _____.

J. Two line dialogues: Read the sentences in A, and find an appropriate response in B.

A		B	
_d_	1. I've got to get away.	a.	Really? I get a kick out of them.
____	2. He was lucky to live through it.	b.	The manager says it's on the house.
____	3. Let's eat out tonight.	c.	Keep in touch.
____	4. I'm sick of his jokes.	d.	Why don't you make plans for a vacation?
____	5. We shouldn't put up with all the problems at the office.	e.	Do you want to go out on a limb and try that new place down the street?
____	6. I'd like to pay for my drink now.	f.	I think it's time to take a stand.
____	7. I'm so sorry your house burned down.	g.	I know. It was a close call.
____	8. I'll catch you later.	h.	It's a very bitter pill to swallow.

Now work with a partner. Role-play the two-line dialogues, adding appropriate body language and intonation.

K. Idiom game: Play this game in pairs or groups of three. Each player should put a different marker (a penny, a button, etc.) on START. Players will take turns, beginning with the person whose birthday comes first in the year.

Directions:

1. When it is your turn close your eyes. Use your pencil to touch a number (in the box on the right). Move your marker that many spaces.

2. Try to make a **personal, true** sentence using the idiom.

3. If you can do it, stay on the space. If you cannot, go back two spaces.

4. The first person to reach FINISH is the winner.

4	3	2	1	2
2	4	3	4	3
1	2	2	3	1

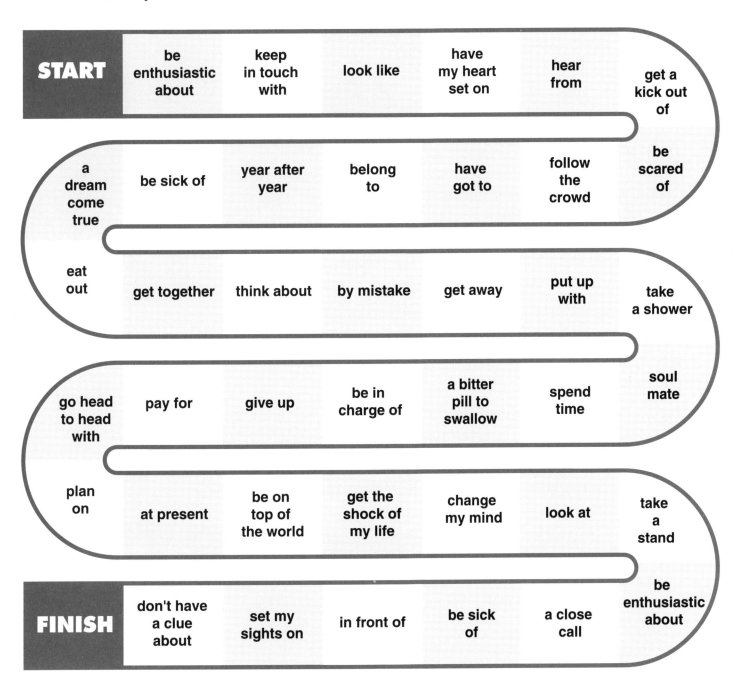

START	be enthusiastic about	keep in touch with	look like	have my heart set on	hear from	get a kick out of
						be scared of
a dream come true	be sick of	year after year	belong to	have got to	follow the crowd	
eat out	get together	think about	by mistake	get away	put up with	take a shower
						soul mate
go head to head with	pay for	give up	be in charge of	a bitter pill to swallow	spend time	
plan on	at present	be on top of the world	get the shock of my life	change my mind	look at	take a stand
						be enthusiastic about
FINISH	don't have a clue about	set my sights on	in front of	be sick of	a close call	

Emu Falls Madly in Love

8

1. Quick Reading

Look at the pictures on page 51.
What is the story about?

Now read quickly to get the main idea.

MOBILE, AL, USA ¹One fall day, a giant bird **showed up at** the home of Ed Stuardi and **fell madly in love with** him. ²He and his wife first saw the six-foot emu drinking water from their bird bath and eating berries from their trees. ³Then Ed began to feed her dog food, not knowing that he was **asking for trouble**. ⁴Soon the bird was following Ed **all day long** and **driving** him **crazy**.

⁵Then things **went from bad to worse**. One day the bird ran toward Ed, making noises deep in her throat. Ed didn't realize these were mating calls. ⁶He **was scared stiff**. Smaller than the bird, Ed tried to **keep** her **away** with a stick.

⁷For two days, Ed didn't dare **go out of** his house. He called the police, but they said they couldn't **help** him **out**. They didn't have the equipment to catch the bird.

⁸Finally, Ed contacted the Animal Rescue Foundation, which **got involved** and caught the bird. Diane Roberts, director of the Foundation, explained the situation this way: "Mr. Stuardi was feeding her and it was mating season. So she had her heart set on this man. Hopefully she'll meet another fellow and forget about Mr. Stuardi. **After all**, he is a married man."

---

mating call: the noise made by an animal when it is looking for love
mating season: the time of year when animals make love

fall madly in love (with someone)	begin to love (someone) very much
show up (at a place)*	arrive (somewhere); appear
ask for trouble	do something that will cause problems later
all day long	during the entire day
drive someone crazy	annoy or irritate someone
go from bad to worse	go from a bad situation to a very bad situation
be scared stiff (of someone or something)	be very afraid (of someone or something)
keep someone or something away*	make someone or something stay at a distance
go out (of a place)*	leave (a place)
help (someone) out*	be helpful (to someone)
get involved (with something)	become active or interested (in something)
after all	one must remember that; consider the fact that

recycled idiom: have one's heart set on   *phrasal verb (see Lexicon and Appendix D)

2. Listen

Cover the story and look only at these pictures. Listen to the story two or three times.

3. Read the Story

Now read the story carefully. Pay special attention to the idioms so that you're ready for Exercise 4.

4. Listen and Complete

Close your book. Listen to the story again. When the tape or your teacher pauses, try to complete the idiom.

5. Match

Complete the idioms using the words in the box. Then write the number of the matching definition.

crazy	stiff	all	trouble
up	involved	long	

_____ *a.* be scared _____   1. annoy or irritate someone

_____ *b.* all day _____   2. do something that will cause a problem

_____ *c.* ask for _____   3. arrive; appear

_____ *d.* drive someone _____   4. become active or interested

_____ *e.* after _____   5. be very afraid

_____ *f.* show _____   6. consider the fact that

_____ *g.* get _____   7. during the entire day

6. Tell the Story

Look only at the pictures and the New Idioms box on page 51. Tell the story using as many idioms as you can.
a. First, work with the whole class to retell the story.
b. Then tell the story to a partner or small group.

7. Answer the Questions

About the story..

a. When did the bird show up at Ed's house?

b. Why did she fall madly in love with Ed?

c. What did she do that drove him crazy?

d. When did things begin to go from bad to worse?

e. How did Ed keep the emu away?

f. What couldn't Ed do for two days?

g. What did the police say when Ed called?

h. Who finally got involved?

About you..

i. Do you have a pet? What kinds of problems does it cause? What do you love about it?

j. Who or what drives you crazy? Why?

k. Tell about a time when you were scared stiff.

l. Who helps you out? Who do you help out?

m. Is there a situation in the world right now that is going from bad to worse? Discuss your ideas with the class.

8. Take a Dictation

Listen to the tape or your teacher and write the dictation in your notebook.

9. Complete the Idioms

a. Yasuko was scared _____ when she went _____ of her tent and saw a bear.

b. Ravi was asking _____ when he started fixing his engine. He worked all day _____, but the leak just went from bad _____.

c. Eva fell madly _____ Eli because of his sense of humor, but now it just drives her _____.

10. Look at Grammar

go out
go out of a place
> *She went out and got in her car.*
> *She went out of the restaurant and got in her car.*

Note: *Go out* and *go out of* mean *leave*. *Go out* can also mean *leave one's house for the purpose of entertainment*, as in *We went out last night and had a great time! Go out* is an intransitive phrasal verb. *Go out of* is transitive and inseparable. See Appendix D for more information on phrasal verbs.

help out
help out with something
help someone out with something
> *Jin's parents help out whenever they can.*
> *Jin's parents help out with the baby whenever they can.*
> *Jin's parents help her out with the baby whenever they can.*

Note: *Help out* can be intransitive or transitive and separable. See Appendix D for more information on phrasal verbs.

fall madly in love
fall madly in love with someone
be madly in love
be madly in love with someone
> *Last summer, Esmeralda fell madly in love for the first time.*
> *She fell madly in love with Diego and married him.*
> *They're still madly in love.*
> *They're still madly in love with each other.*

Note: *Fall madly in love* is a stronger way of saying *fall in love*. A similar expression is *fall head over heels in love*. In these expressions *fall* means *begin*. *Be in love with someone* means *love someone very much*.

Complete the sentences with help from the grammar box above. Make sure they are true for you.

a. I often help _____ out _____,

   and _____ helps me _____.

b. At the age of _____, I fell madly _____

   _____.

c. Before I go _____ my house/apartment, I always _____

   _____.

d. I _____ go _____ on weekends.

11. Write a Dialogue

Work with a partner. Write a dialogue using at least four idioms from the unit.
Act it out for the class.

12. Complete the Story

a. Fill in the blanks in this true story with idioms from the box. Put the verbs in the correct form and tense.

- after all
- go from bad to worse (v)
- help out (v)
- scared stiff
- ask for trouble (v)
- show up (v)

Gorilla Helps Police Out

JOHANNESBURG, SOUTH AFRICA **Running away*** from police, Isaac Mofokeng tried to hide in the local zoo. He jumped over a low wall into one of the animal cages. He did not know it, but he was (1) _____. The pen

belonged to Max the gorilla, who did not appreciate the unexpected visit.

"The first thing the gorilla did was rip my jeans and bite me," Mofokeng said later in court. The gorilla held Mofokeng against the wall. (2) _____, Mofokeng tried to shoot the gorilla with his pistol, but it was **in vain****.

Things (3) _____ for Mofokeng. "Max then dropped me into the water. He grabbed my leg and swung me around. I thought my last hour had come," he told the court. When the police finally (4) _____, **it's no wonder***** that Mofokeng was happy to see them.

Mofokeng is on trial for robbery and for shooting at a gorilla. Max, meanwhile, has become a local hero. (5) _____, he (6) _____ the police, without even asking for a day's wages.

* run away: try to escape

** in vain: without success

*** it's no wonder: it is not surprising

b. Read or tell the story to a partner.

Man Ties the Knot with Stranger

1. Quick Reading

Look at the pictures on page 57.
What is the story about?

Now read quickly to get the main idea.

MINNEAPOLIS, MN, USA ¹David Weinlick, 28 and still single, **was sick and tired of** the question "When are you going to **get married**?" ²So he set a date for his wedding—June 13—and began to **get ready for** it. He **handed out** wedding invitations, got a tuxedo, and bought the wedding rings.

³There was only one problem: David didn't have a bride. He wasn't even **going out with** anyone! ⁴So he began to organize a bridal contest. It would **take place** on June 13 at a shopping mall, and he would marry the winner immediately afterwards. He invited his friends and relatives to come and choose the perfect wife for him. ⁵Some people thought he **was out of his mind**, but only his father refused the invitation. "I think a bridal contest **makes light of** something serious," he said.

⁶On June 13, the wedding day, 25 single women showed up at the mall. David's friends interviewed the women and then they voted. ⁷The winner was Elizabeth Runze, who, like David, is a student at the University of Minnesota. Moments later, Elizabeth and David **tied the knot**. The lucky bride **was flying high**. "This is the most incredible day of my life," Elizabeth told the crowd of friends, shoppers, and reporters. ⁸David is happy too. He and his new bride have **hit it off**. "She is marvelous," he says.

tie the knot (with someone) · · · ·	marry (someone)
be sick and tired of something · ·	feel unable to tolerate something any longer
get married (to someone) · · · · · ·	marry (someone)
get ready (for something) · · · · ·	prepare (for something)
hand something out* · · · · · · · · ·	distribute something
go out with someone* · · · · · · · ·	have a romance with someone; go somewhere with a friend
take place · · · · · · · · · · · · · · · · · ·	happen
be out of one's mind · · · · · · · · ·	be crazy, irrational, silly
make light of something · · · · · ·	act as if something is unimportant
be flying high · · · · · · · · · · · · · · ·	be very happy
hit it off (with someone) · · · · · ·	quickly become good friends (with someone)

recycled idiom: show up   *phrasal verb (see Lexicon and Appendix D)

📼 **2. Listen**

Cover the story and look only at these pictures. Listen to the story two or three times.

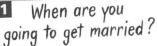

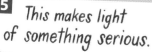

3. Read the Story

Now read the story carefully. Pay special attention to the idioms so that you're ready for Exercise 4.

📟 4. Listen and Complete

Close your book. Listen to the story again. When the tape or your teacher pauses, try to complete the idiom.

5. Match

Complete the idioms using the words in the box. Then write the number of the matching definition.

| one's mind | the knot | and tired of | it off |
| high | ready for | light of | |

_____ **a.** tie _____   **1.** be very happy

_____ **b.** hit _____   **2.** unable to tolerate any longer

_____ **c.** make _____   **3.** marry

_____ **d.** be sick _____   **4.** be crazy or irrational

_____ **e.** get _____   **5.** prepare for

_____ **f.** be out of _____   **6.** quickly become good friends

_____ **g.** be flying _____   **7.** act as if something is unimportant

6. Tell the Story

Look only at the pictures and the New Idioms box on page 57. Tell the story using as many idioms as you can.
a. First, work with the whole class to retell the story.
b. Then tell the story to a partner or small group.

7. **Answer the Questions**

About the story . . . .

a. Why did David Weinlick decide to get married?

b. What did he do to get ready for his wedding?

c. What was David's one big problem?

d. When did the bridal competition take place?

e. What did his friends think about David's plan?

f. Why did his father refuse to come?

g. Who showed up?

h. Who was the winner? How did she feel?

i. What do you think of David's wedding? Was he out of his mind?

About you . . . .

j. Are you married? If not, are you going out with someone? Do you want to tie the knot?

k. Has anyone ever told you that you were out of your mind?

l. What kind of people do you hit it off with?

m. Tell about a time when you were flying high.

n. What job do you have in mind for your future? How can you get ready for the job?

o. What are you sick and tired of?

8. **Take a Dictation**

Listen to the tape or your teacher and write the dictation in your notebook.

9. **Complete the Idioms**

a. Petra and Boris just tied the _____ and they're flying _____.

b. Jared went _____ with his girlfriend last night to a party, which took _____ at the Red Hot Pepper Club.

c. The teacher is handing _____ a test which her students are getting _____ to take.

10. Look at Grammar

hit it off
hit it off with someone
  Mary and I really hit it off.
  I really hit it off with Mary.

Note: This expression is often used in the past tense, as in the above examples. Remember that the past tense of *hit* is *hit*.

be sick and tired of something
be sick and tired of doing something
  I'm sick and tired of that loud music.
  I'm sick and tired of hearing that loud music.

Note: The expressions *be sick of* and *be tired of* are similar in meaning to *be sick and tired of*, but are not quite as strong.

get ready
get ready for something
get ready to do something
  I'm getting ready!
  I'm getting ready for the party.
  I'm getting ready to go to the party.

hand out something / **hand** something **out**
hand out something **to** someone / **hand** something **out to** someone
  She handed out her business cards. She handed her business cards out.
  She handed out her business cards to everyone. She handed her business cards out to everyone.
  She handed them out to everyone.

Note: *Hand out* is a phrasal verb. It is transitive and separable. Remember that the pronoun must occur between the two parts of the phrasal verb when the verb is separable. See Appendix D for more information on phrasal verbs.

Complete the sentences with help from the grammar box above. Make sure they are true for you.

a. When I met _____ I really hit it off _____

 because _____ .

b. I'm sick and tired _____ .

c. In the morning, I get ready for _____ .

d. I need to get ready to _____ .

e. This week, my teacher handed _____

 out to _____ .

11. Write a Dialogue

Work with a partner. Write a dialogue using at least four idioms from the unit.
Act it out for the class.

12. Complete the Story

a. Fill in the blanks in this true story with idioms from the box. Put the verbs in the correct form and tense.

- tie the knot (v)
- get ready (v)
- out of their minds
- show up (v)
- hit it off (v))
- take place (v)

Couple Has Wedding in the Skies

Perris, CA, USA Scott Gehrke and Lorrie Kilgore met while they were taking skydiving lessons. They (1)_____. immediately. A year later they decided to (2)_____ —in the sky!

On their wedding day, they went up in a plane with a parachuting preacher and (3)_____ to jump. The ceremony (4)_____ as they fell 13,000 feet (3962 meters). Preacher Rick Lemons used hand signals to conduct the one-minute ceremony in the skies. The bride and groom kissed before pulling the ripcords on their parachutes. About 100 friends and family members (5)_____ to watch from the ground, including Kilgore's two daughters from a previous marriage.

Afterwards, the bride and groom **were all smiles***. Some people thought they were (6)_____, but Kilgore, 31, said, "We are rebels. This made sense to us. We **fell for*** each other, literally!

* be all smiles: be very happy (informal)

** fall for someone: fall in love with someone (informal)

b. Read or tell the story to a partner.

10 Graffiti Makes Him See Red

1. Quick Reading

Look at the pictures on page 63.
What is the story about?

Now read quickly to get the main idea.

Mike Quintana hates graffiti.

DENVER, CO, USA **1**Mike Quintana **can't stand** graffiti. It makes him **see red**. **2**Quintana owns Sloan Lake Gym in Denver. Like other business owners there, he spends a lot of time trying to **get rid of** the graffiti on his walls. "It takes business owners all their lives to build something. Then punks come to their buildings and put their names **all over the place**. It's demoralizing," says Quintana. **3**Quintana also tries to **do away with** graffiti in his neighborhood. A few times a week, he drives around **looking for** new graffiti. He paints over the graffiti on park benches, garbage cans, and walls.

4One recent evening, Quintana heard a noise outside his gym and **caught** three teens **red-handed.** They were spray painting graffiti on his building. **5**He pulled one teen into the gym, and the other two followed. There was a fight. **6**Somehow Quintana **got the upper hand** and called the police, who put the teens in handcuffs. Then one of the teens threatened to kill Quintana. **7That was the last straw**. Quintana **hit the ceiling**. He grabbed a can of red paint and sprayed two of the boys in the face.

8Now Quintana is **paying the price for losing his cool.** He was arrested, convicted of assault, and sentenced to 40 hours of community service. "Two wrongs don't make a right," said the judge.

---

punks: young people who commit petty crimes
convicted of assault: found guilty of trying to do physical harm to someone

New idioms and expressions

see red	be very angry
can't stand something	dislike something very much
get rid of something	remove; throw something away
all over the place	everywhere
do away with something*	put an end to something; destroy something
look for someone or something*	try to find someone or something
catch someone red-handed	catch someone in the act of doing something wrong
get the upper hand	get the power or advantage
That's the last straw!	After so many problems, that's just too much to endure!
hit the ceiling	become very angry
pay the price (for something)	receive punishment (for something)
lose one's cool	get angry; lose one's temper

recycled idiom: spend time   **phrasal verb (see Lexicon and Appendix D)*

▭ 2. Listen

Cover the story and look only at these pictures. Listen to the story two or three times.

3. Read the Story

Now read the story carefully. Pay special attention to the idioms so that you're ready for Exercise 4.

4. Listen and Complete

Close your book. Listen to the story again. When the tape or your teacher pauses, try to complete the idiom.

5. Match

Complete the idioms using the words in the box. Then write the number of the matching definition.

hand	price	rid of	red
red-handed	straw	stand	

_____ **a.** see _____   **1.** achieve the advantage

_____ **b.** get _____   **2.** dislike something very much

_____ **c.** get the upper _____   **3.** catch in the act of doing something wrong

_____ **d.** can't _____   **4.** too much to endure

_____ **e.** the last _____   **5.** remove; throw away

_____ **f.** pay the _____   **6.** receive punishment for something

_____ **g.** catch _____   **7.** be angry

6. Tell the Story

Look only at the pictures and the New Idioms box on page 63. Tell the story using as many idioms as you can.
a. First, work with the whole class to retell the story.
b. Then tell the story to a partner or small group.

7. Answer the Questions

About the story..

a. How does Quintana feel about graffiti?

b. What does he do about the graffiti on the gym walls?

c. What does he do about graffiti in the neighborhood?

d. What happened after Quintana heard a noise outside his gym?

e. What was the last straw for him?

f. What did he do when he hit the ceiling?

g. What price is Quintana paying for losing his cool?

h. Do you think Quintana deserved his punishment? Why or why not?

About you..

i. How do you feel about graffiti? Is it vandalism or street art, in your opinion?

j. Is graffiti all over the place in your neighborhood? If yes, should you and your neighbors do something about it? What?

k. What makes you lose your cool?

l. What can't you stand?

m. If you could, what would you do away with in the world?

8. Take a Dictation

Listen to the tape or your teacher and write the dictation in your notebook.

9. Complete the Idioms

a. When Jose heard the bad news, it was the last _____. He lost his _____.

b. Mrs. Lorenzo cleaned her son's apartment and did _____ with years of dust and dirt. She got _____ all his old clothes, old food, and old papers.

c. Tina painted pictures all over _____ in her house—on the floor, on the walls, even on the furniture. Her father caught her _____ and hit the _____.

10. Look at Grammar

get the upper hand
get the upper hand on someone
get the upper hand by doing something
> *Pierre is always trying to get the upper hand.*
> *Pierre is always trying to get the upper hand on me.*
> *Then I try to get the upper hand by ignoring him.*

pay the price
pay the price for something
pay the price for doing something
> *She committed a crime, and she'll have to pay the price.*
> *I had to pay the price for my mistake.*
> *I had to pay the price for making a big mistake.*

get rid of something
do away with something
> *I got rid of my old car and bought a new one.*
> *The company is trying to do away with energy waste.*

Note: These two expressions are very close in meaning and are often used interchangeably: *She wants to get rid of government corruption; She wants to do away with government corruption.* However, *get rid of* can also mean *throw away,* for example, *I got rid of the garbage.*

Complete the sentences with help from the grammar box above. Make sure they are true for you.

a. In my neighborhood, I'd like to do away _____ .

b. I'd like to get rid _____ in the world.

c. When I was younger, I had to pay the price _____

_____ .

d. When I was growing up in my family, _____ often tried to get the

upper hand _____ .

11. Write a Dialogue
Work with a partner. Write a dialogue using at least four idioms from the unit.
Act it out for the class.

12. Complete the Dialogue

a. Two co-workers are talking at their computers.
Fill in the blanks with idioms from the box.
Put the verbs in the correct form and tense.

> • **get rid of** (v)
> • **the last straw**
> • **look for** (v)
> • **lose your cool** (v)
> • **hit the ceiling** (v)
> • **can't stand** (v)

Oh, no. I don't believe this. This is really
(1)_____ !

What's wrong now?

I just lost all my data. I'll have to **start from scratch***. I
(2)_____ this computer.

Don't (3)_____! I'll help
you get it back.

I don't think you can. The data's gone.

Let me try! I'll (4)_____ it.

I should just (5)_____ this dinosaur. It's
time for a **brand new**** computer.

It's time for a new attitude. You need to learn patience. You
can't (6)_____ every time there's a
little problem.

* start from scratch: start from the beginning

** brand new: completely new

b. Work with a partner. Role-play the dialogue together.

Family Hits the Road with a Horse, a Wagon, and a Dream

1. Quick Reading

Look at the pictures on page 69.
What is the story about?

Now read quickly to get the main idea.

ORKNEY ISLANDS, SCOTLAND ¹Like many people, David and Kate Grant **dreamed of** going around the world. But their dream was **out of the ordinary**—the Grants and their three children wanted to travel in a horse-drawn wagon! "It started as **a pipe dream**," says David. "None of us knew a thing about driving a horse."

²In 1990, the Grants sold their house in Scotland, bought a horse and wagon, and **hit the road**. They brought along a set of encyclopedias so the children could **keep up with** their studies.

³The trip **got off to a good start** as the family rode through Belgium, France, and Italy. ⁴But then they **ran into** some problems. They arrived in Slovenia in 1991 at the start of the Balkan wars, just as jets were bombing the country.

⁵Two years later, in 1993, after crossing Hungary, Russia, and Kazakhstan, **red tape** prevented them from entering China. ⁶They had to go 1600 kilometers **out of their way** into Mongolia. There, thieves tried to rob them, and the Grants used a slingshot to **drive** them **away**.

⁷In 1996, the family flew from Japan to North America for **the last leg** of their trip. They spent more than a year crossing the United States and Canada. ⁸In late 1997, after seven years **on the road**, the family sailed from Nova Scotia back to Scotland. Kate says she's ready to **settle down** now, but David is not so sure. "Maybe I've got another expedition in me," he says.

Balkan wars: wars that began with the breakup of the former Yugoslavia
slingshot: a forked stick with an elastic band used to shoot small stones
expedition: an adventurous trip or journey that has a specific purpose

New idioms and expressions

hit the road	leave, start a trip (usually in a car)
dream of (doing) something*	think about something that you wish for the future
out of the ordinary	unusual; different
a pipe dream	an unrealistic plan
keep up (with someone or something)*	maintain the pace (of someone or something)
get off to a good start	have a successful beginning
run into someone or something*	meet someone or something unexpectedly
red tape	unnecessary bureaucratic routines
out of one's way	not in the direction one is going
drive someone away*	force someone to leave
the last leg	the final stage of a trip
on the road	traveling; moving from one place to another
settle down*	begin to live a stable life in one place

recycled idiom: spend time   *phrasal verb (see Lexicon and Appendix D)

2. Listen

Cover the story and look only at these pictures. Listen to the story two or three times.

3. Read the Story

Now read the story carefully. Pay special attention to the idioms so that you're ready for Exercise 4.

4. Listen and Complete

Close your book. Listen to the story again. When the tape or your teacher pauses, try to complete the idiom.

5. Match

Complete the idioms using the words in the box. Then write the number of the matching definition.

ordinary	leg	tape	down
the road	dream	a good start	

_____ **a.** the last _____   **1.** unnecessary bureaucratic routines

_____ **b.** out of the _____   **2.** the final stage of a trip

_____ **c.** a pipe _____   **3.** have a successful beginning

_____ **d.** red _____   **4.** an unrealistic plan

_____ **e.** hit _____   **5.** leave; start a car trip

_____ **f.** settle _____   **6.** unusual; different

_____ **g.** get off to _____   **7.** begin to live a stable life in one place

6. Tell the Story

Look only at the pictures and the New Idioms box on page 69. Tell the story using as many idioms as you can.

a. First, work with the whole class to retell the story.

b. Then tell the story to a partner or small group.

7. Answer the Questions

a. What did the Grants dream of doing?

b. Why was their dream out of the ordinary?

c. When did they hit the road? How long were they on the road?

d. How did the children keep up with their studies?

e. What problems did they run into?

f. Why couldn't they enter China?

g. How far out of their way was Mongolia? What happened there?

h. What was the last leg of their trip?

i. Are the Grants ready to settle down now?

j. Would you like to go around the world as the Grants did? Why/why not?

A b o u t   y o u ....

k. Do you like to be on the road? Tell about the last time you hit the road.

l. Tell about something you've done that is out of the ordinary.

m. Tell what you know about the wars in the Balkans.

n. What do you dream of doing? Is it a pipe dream or is it realistic?

o. Is it hard for you to keep up with anything in your life (such as your studies, your e-mail messages, housecleaning, laundry, etc.)?

8. Take a Dictation

Listen to the tape or your teacher and write the dictation in your notebook.

9. Complete the Idioms

a. For many years, Selma and her husband dreamed _____ walking through Australia. It wasn't a pipe _____! They're now on the last _____ of their trip through that country.

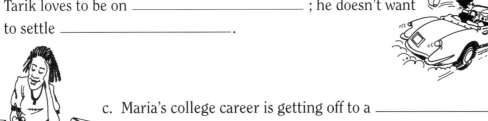

b. Tarik loves to be on _____ ; he doesn't want to settle _____.

c. Maria's college career is getting off to a _____: she's studying hard and keeping _____ with her courses.

10. Look at Grammar

dream of something
dream of doing something

Chang is dreaming of a long vacation in Hawaii.
Chang is dreaming of taking a long vacation in Hawaii.

Note: This phrasal verb is transitive and inseparable. For more information on phrasal verbs, see Appendix D.

keep up
keep up with someone
keep up with something

School is hard for Mindy; it's difficult for her to keep up.
School is hard for Mindy; it's difficult for her to keep up with the other children.
School is hard for Mindy; it's difficult for her to keep up with math and reading.

Note: *Keep up* is an intransitive phrasal verb. *Keep up with* is transitive and inseparable. For more information on phrasal verbs, see Appendix D.

settle down

In the past ten years, I've had five different jobs and lived in five different cities.
Now it's time for me to settle down.

Note: You can also settle down *with someone*, settle down *in a place*, and settle down *and do something* (get married, have a family, get a steady job, etc.) *Settle down* is an intransitive phrasal verb. See Appendix D for more information on phrasal verbs.

Complete the sentences with help from the grammar box above. Make sure they are true for you.

a. When I'm older, I would like to settle _____ in _____

   and (do what?) _____ .

b. It's not easy for me to keep up _____

   because _____ .

c. I often dream _____ someday

   because _____ .

11. Write a Dialogue

Work with a partner. Write a dialogue using at least four idioms from the unit.
Act it out for the class.

12. Complete the Dialogue

a. Luisa and Antonio are a married couple talking about their next vacation. Fill in the blanks with idioms from the box. Put the verbs in the correct form and tense.

> • settle down (v)
> • hit the road (v)
> • keep up with (v)
> • dream of (v)
> • out of the ordinary
> • on the road
> • run into (v)

Honey, look at this brochure about the Colorado River.

Oh, no. What are you (1) _____ now?

I want to (2) _____ next summer and do something fun. Something (3) _____. This would be perfect!

What do you mean, perfect?

Well, we could raft for a week on the river!

No, the Colorado River is too dangerous. We could (4) _____ problems.

Antonio, you're so boring! You never want to do anything.

And all you want to do is go, go, go. You always want to be (5) _____.

Is that bad?

No, darling, but it's hard for me to (6) _____ you. I want a quiet vacation **for a change***. You know I like to (7) _____ in one place and just **chill out****.

* for a change: for once; for something different

** chill out: relax (informal)

b. Work with a partner. Role-play the dialogue together.

A One-of-a-Kind Hotel

12

1. Quick Reading

Look at the pictures on page 75.
What is the story about?

Now read quickly to get the main idea.

KEY LARGO, FL, USA **1**Jules' Undersea Lodge in Key Largo is a **one-of-a-kind** hotel. It is completely underwater! It sits on legs at the bottom of a 30-foot-deep lagoon, completely underwater. To **check in**, you have to scuba dive and enter through a hole under the hotel. **2**This hole leads to a "wet" room where you **take off** your wet clothes and **dry off.**

3The underwater hotel is comfortable. There are books, videos, hot showers, and also phones so you can keep in touch with people on land. **4**Each of the two bedrooms has a big window where you can watch hundreds of fish **go by.** When you **wake up**, you may see an angelfish or parrotfish watching you. "It's a moment you'll never forget," says Ian Koblick, an underwater scientist. **5**For special occasions, the hotel **gives you the red-carpet treatment.** A chef can scuba dive to the hotel and cook a special meal for you. A birthday cake or flowers can also be delivered.

6A control room on land monitors the hotel **at all times.** It pumps fresh air into the hotel and **keeps** water **out**. **7**You can explore the ocean attached to a long line, which provides a limitless air supply. But if diving is **not your cup of tea,** you can relax inside the hotel.

8Yes, you'll **pay through the nose for** a night at Jules' Lodge ($325 per person), but you'll **have a ball**. "To live beneath the sea was once just a science fiction fantasy. Now it is a reality," says owner Dr. Neil Monney.

---

lagoon: a shallow body of water near a lake or ocean
monitor: watch or check carefully

An unusual place to spend the night, Jules' Undersea Lodge.

one-of-a-kind ·	unique; one that does not exist elsewhere
check in* ·	register at a hotel, a convention, a hospital, etc.
take something off* · · · · · · · · · · · · · · · · ·	remove something (clothing, jewelry, makeup, a cover from a jar, etc.)
dry off* ·	become dry
go by (someone or something)* · · · · · · ·	pass; move past (someone or something)
wake up* ·	awaken from sleep
give someone the red-carpet treatment ·	welcome a guest with special attention
at all times ·	constantly; continuously
keep someone or something out* · · · · ·	not allow someone or something to enter
not one's cup of tea · · · · · · · · · · · · · · · · ·	not something one enjoys
pay through the nose (for something) ·	pay a very high price (for something)
have a ball ·	have a wonderful time; really enjoy oneself

recycled idiom: keep in touch   *phrasal verb (see Lexicon and Appendix D)

🔲 **2. Listen**

Cover the story and look only at these pictures. Listen to the story two or three times.

3. Read the Story

Now read the story carefully. Pay special attention to the idioms so that you're ready for Exercise 4.

4. Listen and Complete

Close your book. Listen to the story again. When the tape or your teacher pauses, try to complete the idiom.

5. Match

Complete the idioms using the words in the box. Then write the number of the matching definition.

a ball	the nose	kind	treatment
by	in		of tea

_____ **a.** one-of-a-_____ 1. not something one enjoys

_____ **b.** not one's cup _____ 2. pass

_____ **c.** give the red-carpet _____ 3. register at a hotel

_____ **d.** have _____ 4. welcome a guest with special attention

_____ **e.** go _____ 5. pay a very high price

_____ **f.** pay through _____ 6. unique

_____ **g.** check _____ 7. really enjoy oneself

6. Tell the Story

Look only at the pictures and the New Idioms box on page 75. Tell the story using as many idioms as you can.

a. First, work with the whole class to retell the story.

b. Then tell the story to a partner or small group.

7. Answer the Questions

About the story . . . .

a. Why is Jules' Lodge one-of-a-kind?

b. What do you have to do to check into the hotel?

c. What do you do in the "wet" room?

d. What goes by outside the hotel window?

e. In what ways does the hotel give you the red-carpet treatment?

f. How does the control room keep you safe?

g. How can you spend your time if diving is not your cup of tea?

h. Is the hotel expensive?

i. Would you have a ball at this hotel? Why/why not?

About you . . . .

j. Imagine a special place you want to go. What do you see when you wake up? What goes by your window?

k. Describe a place where you had a ball.

l. Do you own anything that is one-of-a-kind? Describe it.

m. Have you ever given the red-carpet treatment to a guest in your house? What did you do?

n. What sports or activities are not your cup of tea?

8. Take a Dictation

Listen to the tape or your teacher and write the dictation in your notebook.

9. Complete the Idioms

a. Shen paid through _____ for his new boat and then discovered that sailing was not really his cup _____ .

b. The Palace Hotel gives its guests the red-_____ . When you check _____ , they give you a bottle of wine. When you wake _____ , they'll bring you breakfast in bed.

c. Natasha took _____ her wet clothes and is drying _____ by the fire.

10. Look at Grammar

wake up
wake up someone
wake someone **up**
> *Usually Jamal wakes up around 7:00 a.m.*
> *Then he wakes up his children.*
> *Then he wakes his children up.*
> *Then he wakes them up.*

Note: *Wake up* and *wake someone up* are phrasal verbs. *Wake up* is intransitive; *wake someone up* is transitive and separable. Remember that when you use a pronoun (*us, her, you, etc.*) with a separable phrasal verb, it must go between the verb and the particle. See Appendix D for more information on phrasal verbs.

take off something
take something **off**
> *I want to take off these uncomfortable shoes.*
> *I want to take these uncomfortable shoes off.*
> *I want to take them off.*

Note: You can take off *clothing*, take off *a price tag*, take off *a bottle top*, take off *a book cover*, take off *a tablecloth*, take off *a sheet*, etc. *Take something off* is a phrasal verb, and it is transitive and separable. See Appendix D for more information on phrasal verbs.

keep out something or someone
keep something or someone **out**
> *Keep out the mosquitoes. Close the window!*
> *Keep the mosquitoes out. Close the window!*

Note: *Keep out* is a phrasal verb. It is transitive and separable. See Appendix D for more information on phrasal verbs.

Complete the sentences with help from the grammar box above. Make sure they are true for you.

a. I usually wake _____ .

b. I think we should keep _____ out of _____ .

c. My favorite article of clothing is _____ . I don't

   like to take _____ !

d. I take my sheets _____ the bed _____ .

11. Write a Dialogue

Work with a partner. Write a dialogue using at least four idioms from the unit.
Act it out for the class.

12. Complete the Dialogue

a. Leonid is traveling, and he has just arrived at a new hotel. Fill in the blanks with idioms from the box. Put the verbs in the correct form and tense.

> - **give you the red-carpet treatment** (v)
> - **have a ball** (v)
> - **wake...up** (v)
> - **go by** (v)
> - **not my cup of tea**
> - **check in** (v)
> - **at all times**

Hi, I'd like to (1) _____.
My name is Bodnia.

Sure. I'll check your reservation. Yes, you're in Room 301. Here's your key Mr. Bodnia.

Thanks. Will you (2) _____ me _____ at 6:00 a.m. tomorrow?

Sure. We'll **give** you **a call***.

And are there restaurants in the hotel?

Yes, we have two. Our dining room is closed now, but the cafe is open (3) _____.

Great. Where's the cafe?

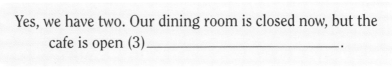

(4) _____ the elevators. Then turn left and go down the stairs. Oh, and **by the way****, there's a good Mexican restaurant next door. They'll (5) _____. There's mariachi music until midnight. It's a great place; you'll (6) _____ !

Thanks, but that's (7) _____.
I'll try your cafe for something quick.

* give someone a call: telephone someone

** by the way: incidentally; while I think of it

b. Work with a partner. Role-play the dialogue together.

Cyber-Romance Leads to Cross-Cultural Marriage

13

1. Quick Reading

Look at the pictures on page 81.
What is the story about?

Now read quickly to get the main idea.

PHILADELPHIA, PA, USA ¹Until recently, Figen Gencosmanoglu, 36, was living in Trabzon, a small town in Turkey. Dan Haigh, 42, was in Philadelphia. Both **were in the same boat**—divorced and lonely. ²They met on the Internet and started e-mailing each other. Figen told Dan all her secrets. "He was so far away, he seemed unreal," she says. "It was like talking to an advice column, but I knew we **had a lot in common**." ³Dan was soon e-mailing Figen three times a day — morning, noon, and night. **Before long,** he wrote, "I'm coming to Turkey." He hadn't even seen a picture of her!

⁴Meanwhile, Figen got a photo of Dan in the mail. It **took ages** for her to open the envelope. She put it on her heart and repeated, "Oh, God, please God." She was already madly in love with him and didn't want to **be disappointed by** the photo. She was not.

⁵A month later, Dan **made the** long and expensive **trip** to Trabzon, his first trip outside the U.S. He **was nervous about** the meeting. On the plane, his mother's words echoed in his head. "What are you doing? **Are** you **nuts**?" In Turkey, Figen **was on edge** too. "Aren't there any American women for him?" her parents had said. ⁶But when Figen and Dan **set eyes on** each other, they knew it **was the real thing**.

⁷Dan researched Turkish marriage customs, and several months later went back to Turkey with his parents and formally **asked for Figen's hand**. ⁸"When you meet on the Internet, you begin as friends. You can really listen to the other person. You have time to think about their words and to **read between the lines**," says Figen, now living happily with Dan near Philadelphia.

---

echo: repeat a sound again and again

New idioms and expressions

be in the same boat (as someone) ·········	be in the same situation, with the same problem(s)
have a lot in common (with someone) ·····	be similar in many ways (to someone)
before long ·····································	in a short time; soon
take ages ·······································	take a long time
be disappointed by someone or something ·	feel that your hopes were not met by someone or something
make a trip ·····································	travel someplace
be nervous about something ··············	feel afraid and a little excited about something
be nuts ···	be crazy, insane
be on edge ·····································	be nervous
set eyes on someone or something ········	see someone or something for the first time
be the real thing ····························	be genuine and authentic
ask for someone's hand ···················	ask for permission to marry someone
read between the lines ····················	guess at something that has not been stated directly

recycled idioms: be madly in love with someone, go back   *phrasal verb (see Lexicon and Appendix D)

2. Listen

Cover the story and look only at these pictures. Listen to the story two or three times.

3. Read the Story

Now read the story carefully. Pay special attention to the idioms so that you're
ready for Exercise 4.

4. Listen and Complete

Close your book. Listen to the story again. When the tape or your teacher pauses,
try to complete the idiom.

5. Match

Complete the idioms using the words in the box. Then write the number of the
matching definition.

boat	edge	eyes on	ages
long	in common	thing	lines

_____ a. have a lot _____ 1. take a long time

_____ b. be in the same _____ 2. see for the first time

_____ c. read between the _____ 3. in a short time; soon

_____ d. before _____ 4. be nervous

_____ e. take _____ 5. be similar in many ways

_____ f. set _____ 6. have the same problems

_____ g. be on _____ 7. be genuine and authentic

_____ h. be the real _____ 8. guess at something that has not
                                          been stated directly

6. Tell the Story

Look only at the pictures and the New Idioms box on page 81. Tell the story using as many
idioms as you can.
a. First, work with the whole class to retell the story.
b. Then tell the story to a partner or small group.

7. Answer the Questions

About the story . . . .

a. Why were Figen and Dan in the same boat?

b. What did Figen realize soon after she and Dan met on the Internet?

c. Why did it take ages for her to look at Dan's photo?

d. When Dan made the trip to Trabzon, how did he feel? Why?

e. How did Figen feel just before he arrived?

f. What happened when they set eyes on each other?

g. Why did Dan go back to Turkey later with his parents?

h. Why does Figen feel that dating on the Internet is a good thing?

About you . . . .

i. Have you met interesting people on the Internet?

j Do you have any friends who are in the same boat as Figen and Dan were? Do you have any advice for them?

k. How do you know when love is the real thing?

l. Tell about a trip you made recently. Were you pleased or disappointed by the trip? Tell why.

m. What are you often nervous about? Why?

8. Take a Dictation

Listen to the tape or your teacher and write the dictation in your notebook.

9. Complete the Idioms

a. Mr. and Mrs. Brown were making _____ to Chicago when their train was delayed for 10 hours. Before _____, it became hot and uncomfortable. Passengers were hungry and on _____, but there was nothing they could do. Everyone was in the same _____.

b. The brothers don't have a lot _____. Tim likes sports and the outdoors; Jim likes to stay inside and read.

c. When Polly first set _____ on John, she wasn't at all _____ by what she saw.

10. Look at Grammar

> **X and Y have a lot in common**
> **X has a lot in common with Y**
> *Sung and her son have a lot in common; they both love science and sports.*
> *Sung has a lot in common with her son; they both love science and sports.*
>
> **Note:** You can make various substitutions in this expression, e.g., *have nothing in common, have many things in common, have a few things in common, have quite a lot in common,* etc.
>
> **be disappointed**
> **be disappointed by** someone / **be disappointed in** someone
> **be disappointed by** something / **be disappointed in** something
> *You missed my party; I was so disappointed!*
> *I was disappointed by/in my brother; he didn't show up for my party.*
> *I was disappointed by/in the movie; it was horrible!*
>
> **be in the same boat**
> **be in the same boat as** someone
> *Pierre and Amy are in the same boat; they've both lost their jobs.*
> *Pierre is in the same boat as Amy; he's lost his job, too.*

Complete the sentences with help from the grammar box above. Make sure they are true for you.

a. I'm in the same boat _____ because

_____.

b. I was disappointed _____ because

he/she _____.

c. _____ and I have _____ in common;

we _____.

d. I have nothing in common _____.

11. Write a Dialogue

Work with a partner. Write a dialogue using at least four idioms from the unit.
Act it out for the class.

12. Complete the Story

a. Fill in the blanks in this true story with idioms from the box. Put the verbs in the correct form and tense.

> - ask for her hand (v)
> - take ages (v)
> - have a lot in common (v)
> - be disappointed (v)
> - before long
> - be nervous about (v)
> - make a trip (v)
> - set eyes on (v)
> - be in the same boat (v)

56 Years of Correspondence Leads to Happy Ending

Soldiers, IA, USA In 1942, Colleen Lee was 14 years old and living in Iowa. She had a pen-pal from England, Geoffrey Lake, who was also 14. Writing to each other was a school assignment. The teenagers did not (1) _____. Colleen was an innocent girl who was happy on her father's farm. Geoffrey was **growing up*** in the middle of a war. But the two teens found it easy to write to each other. (2) _____, they were writing almost every day. However, when the war ended in 1945, they both got married and stopped writing.

It (3) _____—almost 40 years—for Geoffrey to start writing to Colleen again. He was happily married, but he wanted to know what had happened to her. When Colleen got his letter, she was delighted, and their correspondence blossomed again. Colleen was married, too, so there was no romance in their letters, only a strong friendship.

In 1992, Colleen's husband died. Then in 1997, Geoffrey's wife died. Now they (4) _____—widowed, lonely and almost 70 years old.

Their letters became romantic, beginning with "My darling" and "My love." Still, the two had never met. After much persuasion from Geoffrey, Colleen agreed to (5) _____ to New York to meet him. Of course, they (6) _____ the meeting because they didn't want to (7) _____. But, according to Geoffrey, when they first (8) _____ each other, they knew it was the real thing. "It was **love at first sight****. There was no tension or shyness." Geoffrey went down on his knees and (9) _____. The couple married in 1998 and they are now living happily in Iowa. "It seems like a fairy tale," Colleen says.

*grow up: become older; reach adulthood
**love at first sight: love that happens when two people first see each other

b. Read or tell the story to a partner.

Solo Sailor Operates on Himself—via E-mail

14

1. Quick Reading

Look at the pictures on page 87.
What is the story about?

CAPE TOWN, SOUTH AFRICA ¹Viktor Yazykov was on **the first leg** of a sailboat race around the world. The Russian was alone in the Atlantic Ocean, 1,000 miles from shore. He **was in his element.**

²But he **was concerned about** his elbow, which he had injured earlier. Every day it was getting redder and larger. He sent an e-mail message to race headquarters. "RIGHT ELBOW DOESN'T LOOK GOOD. IT FEELS DEAD." ³Dr. Dan Carlin in Boston was in charge of providing emergency care for the sailors via computer. "YOU HAVE GOT TO OPERATE ON YOUR ELBOW," he typed. He carefully **laid out** the steps of the surgery. "IT WILL BE PAINFUL," he warned.

⁴**In the middle of** a violent storm, Yazykov began cutting his arm. He **kept a stiff upper lip**, following the doctor's instructions **to the letter**. ⁵Then something **went wrong**. Blood was all over the place, forming a large pool on the floor, rolling with the motion of the boat. ⁶Yazykov knew that if he **passed out**, he'd die. Using his good arm and his teeth, he tied two cords around his arm. The bleeding stopped, but his arm became cold and white, like a piece of rubber. "PLEASE, WHAT SHOULD I DO BEFORE IT'S TOO LATE?" he wrote to Dr. Carlin.

⁷Carlin knew that Yazykov was killing his arm. "TAKE THE CORDS OFF IMMEDIATELY," he wrote back. But the doctor was confused. **Why in the world** was there so much blood? Suddenly, he **put two and two together**. Aspirin! Yazykov had been taking aspirin for weeks and it had made his blood thin. "STOP ALL ASPIRIN," he ordered. ⁸After an anxious ten hours, Dr. Carlin finally heard from Yazykov. He **was out of the woods**. "I AM OK. GETTING STRONGER. THANK YOU FOR YOUR HELP."

Victor Yazykov returns after his misadventure on the high seas.

New idioms and expressions

the first leg	the first part of a trip
be in one's element	be in a happy and comfortable situation
be concerned about someone or something	worry about someone or something
lay something out*	arrange or organize something
in the middle of something	while something is happening; during something
keep a stiff upper lip	be brave and calm in a difficult situation
to the letter	exactly as written or instructed; perfectly
go wrong	fail; not happen as planned
pass out*	lose consciousness; faint
why in the world?	why really? why in fact?
put two and two together	figure something out; reason from the facts
be out of the woods	be out of danger after an illness, injury, or difficult situation

recycled idioms: be in charge of, have got to, all over the place, take something off, hear from

*phrasal verb (see Lexicon and Appendix D)

2. Listen

Cover the story and look only at these pictures. Listen to the story two or three times.

3. Read the Story

Now read the story carefully. Pay special attention to the idioms so that you're ready for Exercise 4.

4. Listen and Complete

Close your book. Listen to the story again. When the tape or your teacher pauses, try to complete the idiom.

5. Match

Complete the idioms using the words in the box. Then write the number of the matching definition.

woods	out	element	wrong
upper lip	world	leg	

____ **a.** pass _____ **1.** be brave and calm

____ **b.** be out of the _____ **2.** be in a happy and comfortable situation

____ **c.** keep a stiff _____ **3.** the first part of a trip

____ **d.** why in the _____ **4.** be out of danger

____ **e.** be in one's _____ **5.** fail; not happen as planned

____ **f.** go _____ **6.** why really

____ **g.** the first _____ **7.** lose consciousness

6. Tell the Story

Look only at the pictures and the New Idioms box on page 87. Tell the story using as many idioms as you can.

a. First, work with the whole class to retell the story.

b. Then tell the story to a partner or small group.

7. Answer the Questions

About the story . . . .

a. Where was Viktor when he became concerned about his elbow?

b. What did the doctor tell him?

c. What did he lay out in his e-mail message?

d. When did Viktor begin the surgery?

e. How did he react while he was cutting his arm?

f. Was he able to follow the doctor's instructions?

g. What went wrong?

h. What would happen if Viktor passed out?

i. What did the doctor tell Viktor to do with the cords on his arm?

j. When did the doctor finally hear from Viktor? How was he?

k. Would you enjoy sailing alone around the world? Why/why not?

About you . . . .

l. Tell about a dangerous situation when you kept a stiff upper lip.

m. Have you ever passed out? What happened?

n. When are you in your element?

o. What are you concerned about these days?

p. When you take a trip (by car, by plane, by boat), what kinds of things can go wrong?

8. Take a Dictation

Listen to the tape or your teacher and write the dictation in your notebook.

9. Complete the Idioms

a. Herve loves playing the drums. When he's in the _____ a concert, he's really in his _____.

b. Everyone was very concerned _____ Katia after her accident, but now she's out of _____.

c. Agim followed the cake recipe to the _____, but everything went _____. The cake burned and had a funny shape.

10. Look at Grammar

be concerned
be concerned about someone
be concerned about something
  I haven't heard from Bill in a long time, and I'm concerned.
  I haven't heard from Bill in a long time, and I'm concerned about him.
  I haven't heard from Bill in a long time, and I'm concerned about his well-being.

go wrong
go wrong with something
  Everything went wrong today at work!
  A lot of things went wrong with our new project.
  Something also went wrong with my computer and fax.
  Luckily, nothing went wrong with my phone.

Note: The subject used with this expression is usually an indefinite pronoun, such as *everything, something, nothing, many things, several things,* etc.

lay out something
lay something **out**
  I laid out my ideas carefully, but no one liked them.
  I laid my ideas out carefully, but no one liked them.

Note: In the above examples, *lay out* means organize and present. You can lay out *plans, ideas, the steps of a process,* and *your thoughts about something. Lay out* also means *spread out,* as in *I laid out the map on the floor.* It is a transitive, separable phrasal verb. For more information on phrasal verbs, see Appendix D.

Complete the sentences with help from the grammar box above. Make sure they are true for you.

a. My last vacation/trip was _____;

  _____ went wrong.

b. The first time I tried _____,

  _____ went wrong.

c. There are many problems in the world. I'm particularly concerned _____

  _____.

d. I'm concerned _____

  because he/she _____.

e. I laid out _____.

11. Write a Dialogue

Work with a partner. Write a dialogue using at least four idioms from the unit.
Act it out for the class.

12. Complete the Story

a. Fill in the blanks in this true story with idioms from the box. Put the verbs in the correct form and tense.

- keep a stiff upper lip (v)
- in the middle of
- why in the world
- lay out (v)
- out of the woods
- go wrong (v)
- be very concerned about (v)

Internet Angels

Ürümqi, China Yongxin Deng, 31, (1) _____ his three-year-old son. The boy, Shao-Shao (whose name means "laughter"), had a very serious and rare heart disease. Deng wanted his son to have surgery, but doctors in China disagreed. (2) _____ should they operate? The boy was too ill and could not live through an operation.

But Deng was determined. He **turned to** the Internet **for help***. He posted a notice: "Seeking Help to Save My Son." He (3) _____ his problem and asked for "any help or information." He received many replies. Strangers from California, whom Deng calls his "Internet Angels," helped to find more than $110,000 for Shao-Shao's surgery.

Deng, who was (4) _____ his graduate studies, quit everything and took his wife and child to Los Angeles. Doctors there told the Dengs that the heart surgery was dangerous. Something could (5) _____. Little Shao-Shao (6) _____ during his three operations. Everything **went well****, and the boy is now (7) _____.

The Dengs were amazed by all the people who helped them out. "How can we thank people whose names we'll never know?" Deng asked. "Now our son is really a 'laughing' boy!"

* turn to someone or something for help: look for help from someone or something
** go well: be successful (the opposite of *go wrong*)
recycled idioms: live through, help out

b. Read or tell the story to a partner.

Review

A. Fill in the bubbles: What are these people saying? Fill in each speech bubble with an appropriate sentence from the box at the bottom of the page.

1.

2.

3.

4.

5.

6.

7.

8.

9.

10.

You're out of the woods now.

We just tied the knot!

I can't stand this anymore. I'm going inside.

This is not your cup of tea!

I paid through the nose, but I love it.

Stop it! You're driving me crazy.

Would you like to go out Friday?

I'm having a ball!

You're out of your mind!

I caught you red-handed.

B. Odd one out: Cross out the word or phrase that does NOT go with the first word.

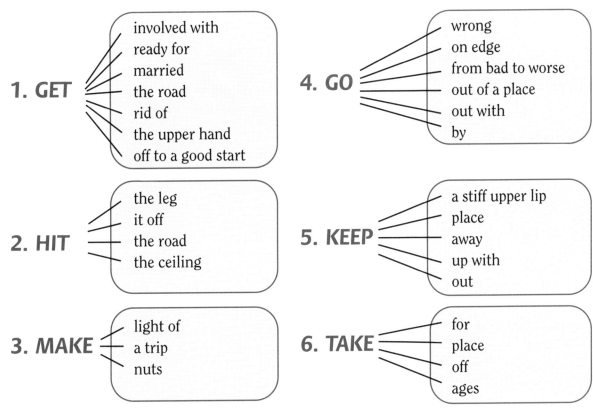

1. GET
- involved with
- ready for
- married
- the road
- rid of
- the upper hand
- off to a good start

4. GO
- wrong
- on edge
- from bad to worse
- out of a place
- out with
- by

2. HIT
- the leg
- it off
- the road
- the ceiling

5. KEEP
- a stiff upper lip
- place
- away
- up with
- out

3. MAKE
- light of
- a trip
- nuts

6. TAKE
- for
- place
- off
- ages

C. Idioms that use *out*: Match the idioms with their definitions.

_____ 1. pass **out**

_____ 2. lay something **out**

_____ 3. go **out** with someone

_____ 4. help **out**

_____ 5. be **out** of one's mind

_____ 6. **out** of the ordinary

_____ 7. hand something **out**

_____ 8. be **out** of the woods

_____ 9. **out** of one's way

_____ 10. go **out** of a place

a. be helpful

b. distribute something

c. lose consciousness

d. arrange something

e. be out of danger

f. leave

g. unusual

h. not in the direction one is going

i. be crazy, irrational

j. have a romance with someone

D. *In* or *on*? Fill in the blanks with *in* or *on*.

1. be _____ one's element

2. be _____ the same boat

3. _____ the road

4. Why _____ the world?

5. be _____ edge

6. _____ the middle of

7. set eyes _____

8. fall madly _____ love with

9. have a lot _____ common with

10. check _____ to a hotel

E. Parts of the body: Many idioms use parts of the body. Finish these idioms with one of the pictured body parts and then match them to their definitions.

_____ 1. the first _____

_____ 2. get the upper _____

_____ 3. keep a stiff upper _____

_____ 4. pay through the _____

_____ 5. ask for someone's _____

_____ 6. set _____ on someone

_____ 7. be out of one's _____

_____ 8. _____ something out

_____ 9. the last _____

a. be crazy, irrational, or silly

b. distribute something

c. get the power or advantage

d. see someone for the first time

e. the beginning of a trip

f. the end of a trip

g. be brave and calm

h. give a lot of money

i. ask permission to marry someone

F. Good or bad? Is the speaker feeling good or bad? Write the sentences in the correct box.

I'm scared stiff.
I'm completely in my element.
This is the last straw!
I feel like I'm going to pass out.
I'm really flying high.
I fell madly in love last night!
I'm seeing red.
We're really hitting it off.

I'm having a ball.
I'm sick and tired of this.
I can't stand this anymore.
I'm on edge.
This is driving me crazy.
Everything's going wrong.
You're giving me the red-carpet treatment.

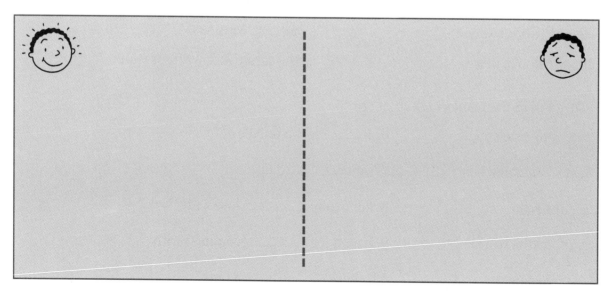

G. Idioms in pictures: Use the pictures to complete the idioms.

1. Maria is _____ ; she spent all her money on a new boat and now she can't pay her rent.

2. I'm really _____. Bobby hasn't called and I'm worried about him.

3. When the boss saw the mistake, he hit the _____.

4. You didn't finish your homework either? We're both in the _____.

5. I don't enjoy skiing; it's just not my _____.

6. Why in the _____ did you get rid of that beautiful chair? I loved it!

7. I just got the job of my dreams. I'm really _____ high!

8. Musa never studied in college. Now he can't graduate and he's really paying the _____.

9. Carmella will never go to China; it's just a _____ dream.

10. Edith has recovered from her illness, and she's now out of _____.

H. Complete the sentences: Complete the sentences so they are true for you.

1. I need to get ready _____.

2. I can't stand movies that _____.

3. People told me I was nuts when I _____.

4. I'll be in my element when _____.

5. When I first set eyes _____ , I felt _____

   because _____.

6. I paid through the nose _____.

7. My _____ is/are one-of-a-kind

   because _____.

8. I sometimes lose my cool when _____.

I. Incorrect ending: Find the sentence ending that is NOT correct and cross it out.

1. I'm getting…
   a. ready for the exam.
   b. rid of my car.
   c. involved with the book committee.
   d. bad to worse.
   e. married tomorrow.

2. Can you keep…
   a. up with your French lessons?
   b. all over the place?
   c. up with George?
   d. the animals away from the garden?

3. I was in…
   a. my element in Tokyo.
   b. the last straw.
   c. the same boat as you.
   d. the middle of dinner when you called.

4. He's really out of…
   a. the ordinary
   b. his mind.
   c. the upper hand.
   d. the woods now.

5. She went out…
   a. of the office at 5:00 PM.
   b. with John last night.
   c. to a good start.
   d. to the movies I think.

J. Idiom game: Play this game in pairs or groups of three. Each player should put a different marker (a penny, a button, etc.) on START. Players will take turns, beginning with the person whose birthday comes first in the year.

Directions:
1. When it is your turn, close your eyes. Use your pencil to touch a number (in the box on the right). Move your marker that many spaces.
2. Try to make a **personal, true** sentence using the idiom.
3. If you can do it, stay on the space. If you cannot, go back two spaces.
4. The first person to reach FINISH is the winner.

4	3	2	1	2
2	4	3	4	3
1	2	2	3	1

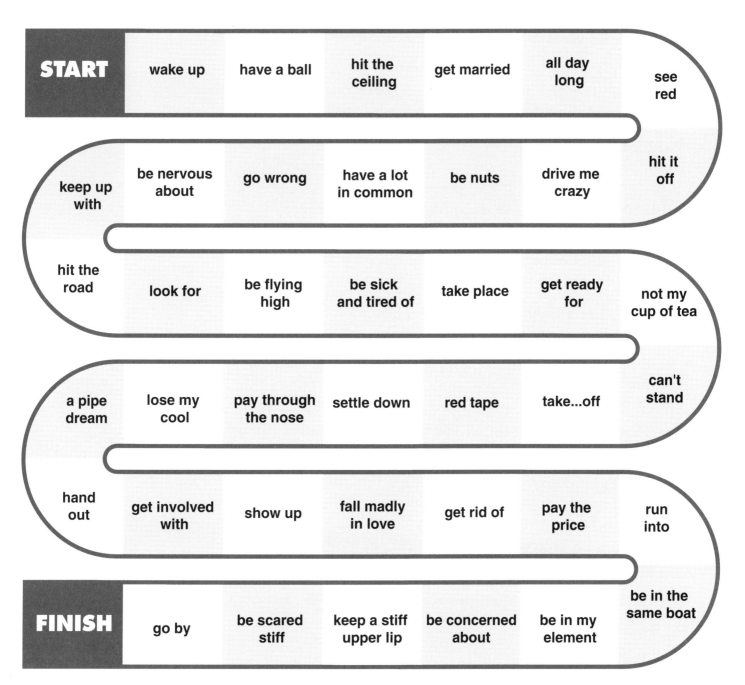

START	wake up	have a ball	hit the ceiling	get married	all day long	see red
						hit it off
keep up with	be nervous about	go wrong	have a lot in common	be nuts	drive me crazy	
hit the road	look for	be flying high	be sick and tired of	take place	get ready for	not my cup of tea
						can't stand
a pipe dream	lose my cool	pay through the nose	settle down	red tape	take...off	
hand out	get involved with	show up	fall madly in love	get rid of	pay the price	run into
						be in the same boat
FINISH	go by	be scared stiff	keep a stiff upper lip	be concerned about	be in my element	

Appendix A: Answer Key

1. Engineer Is Enthusiastic About Odd New Home
page 4: 5) a. hand (5) b. present (7) c. the crowd (1) d. of (6) e. about (3) f. out (2) g. mate (4)

page 5: 8) See Appendix B, page 102.

page 5: 9) a. the crowd, present b. about, on c. for, of

page 7: 12) 1. instead of 2. points out 3. paid...for 4. on the other hand
5. What if 6. are enthusiastic about 7. plan on

2. Man Eats Out and Gets More Than He Ordered
page 10: 5) a. a bear (3) b. the bat (4) c. mistake (6) d. house (7) e. out (1)
f. well as (5) g. back (2)

page 11: 8) See Appendix B, page 102.

page 11: 9) a. a bear, out b. go, house c. mistake, back, on it

page 13: 12) 1. hungry as a bear 2. looked at 3. give back 4. have a clear conscience
5. right off the bat 6. went back 7. as well as

3. Out on a Limb
page 16: 5) a. touch with (5) b. clock (1) c. down (7) d. to head with (4) e. up with (2)
f. stand (3) g. forward to (6)

page 17: 8) See Appendix B, page 102.

page 17: 9) a. the clock, spends b. up with, forward to c. head to head

page 19: 12) 1. going head to head with 2. around the clock 3. going out on a limb
4. According to 5. put up with 6. Keep in touch

4. On Top of the World
page 22: 5) a. attempt (4) b. of the world (1) c. ground (3) d. set on (2) e. to swallow (7)
f. out (5) g. history (6)

page 23: 8) See Appendix B, page 102.

page 23: 9) a. attempt, up b. set on, year out c. made, ground d. up, pill to swallow

page 25: 12) 1. on top of the world 2. Give up 3. had my heart set on 4. year in and year out
5. broke new ground 6. Make an attempt

5. Boy Fights Lion Tooth and Nail
page 28: 5) a. of one's life (5) b. off (6) c. call (1) d. tooth and nail (7) e. charge of (3)
f. glance (4) g. flash (2)

page 29: 8) See Appendix B, page 102.

page 29: 9) a. tooth and nail, go of, off b. in a, call c. of her life, in front

page 31: 12) 1. in charge of 2. set out 3. got the shock of his life 4. In a flash 5. in front of
6. was scared of 7. backed off 8. a close call

6. Face-to-Face After 56 Years

page 34: 5) a. birth to (3) b. down (4) c. after year (7) d. come true (6) e. through (2) f. out (1)
g. pregnant (5)

page 35: 8) See Appendix B, page 102.

page 35: 9) a. together, plans b. birth to, dream, about c. to-face

page 37: 12) 1. gave birth to 2. thought about 3. searched for 4. year after year 5. face-to-face
6. found out 7. a dream come true

7. Globe-Trotting Frog Comes Home

page 40: 5) a. mind (7) b. off (4) c. out of (2) d. line (5) e. sport (6) f. from (3)
g. enough (1)

page 41: 8) See Appendix B, page 102.

page 41: 9) a. mind, clue b. globe-trotting, a kick c. off

page 43: 12) 1. change your mind 2. get away 3. am sick of 4. hear from 5. will drop a line
6. will be back 7. don't have a clue 8. Catch you later

Review: Units 1–7

page 44: A. 1. I don't have a clue. 2. This is a bitter pill to swallow. 3. This is on the house. 4. I'm
sick of this weather. 5. Let go of me! 6. I'm hungry as a bear. 7. This is a dream come
true! 8. I'll catch you later! 9. I'm looking forward to getting away. 10. We're breaking
new ground.

page 45: B. 1. a good sport 2. through 3. down 4. a plan 5. tooth and nail 6. a line

C. 1. e 2. a 3. d 4. b 5. c. 6. g 7. f

D. 1. in 2. on 3. on 4. in 5. in 6. on 7. in 8. on 9. on 10. on 11. on 12. in

page 46: E. 1. hand (e) 2. mind (f) 3. tooth, nail (c) 4. heart (d) 5. head, head (a) 6. face, face (b)

F. Answers will vary.

page 47: G. GOOD: I'm getting a kick out of this; I have a clear conscience; You're my soul mate; It's a
dream come true!; I'm on top of the world.

BAD: Will I live through this?; Someone ripped me off; I can't put up with this anymore;
We're fighting tooth and nail; This is a bitter pill to swallow; I've really got to get away.

H. 1. bear 2. shock 3. clock 4. crowd 5. limb 6. bat

page 48: I. 1. They want to chop it down. 2. Please give it back. 3. I'm searching for them.
4. I didn't look at them. 5. Someone ripped it off. 6. I always think about it. 7. Have
you heard from them yet? 8. Let's take them out. 9. She was careless and burned it
down. 10. Pull into it slowly.

J. 1. d 2. g 3. e 4. a 5. f 6. b 7. h 8. c

page 49: K. Answers will vary.

8. Emu Falls Madly in Love

page 52: 5) a. stiff (5) b. long (7) c. trouble (2) d. crazy (1) e. all (6) f. up (3) g. involved (4)

page 53: 8) See Appendix B, page 102.

page 53: 9) a. stiff, out b. for trouble, long, to worse c. in love with, crazy

page 55: 12) 1. asking for trouble 2. Scared stiff 3. went from bad to worse 4. showed up
5. After all 6. helped out

9. Man Ties the Knot with Stranger

page 58: 5) a. the knot (3)   b. it off (6)   c. light of (7)   d. and tired of (2)   e. ready for (5)
f. one's mind (4)   g. high (1)

page 59: 8) See Appendix B, page 103.

page 59: 9) a. knot, high   b. out, place   c. out, ready

page 61: 12) 1. hit it off   2. tie the knot   3. got ready   4. took place   5. showed up
6. out of their minds

10. Graffiti Makes Him See Red

page 64: 5) a. red (7)   b. rid of (5)   c. hand (1)   d. stand (2)   e. straw (4)   f. price (6)
g. red-handed (3)

page 65: 8) See Appendix B, page 103.

page 65: 9) a. straw, cool   b. away, rid of   c. the place, red-handed, ceiling

page 67: 12) 1. the last straw   2. can't stand   3. lose your cool/hit the ceiling   4. look for
5. get rid of   6. lose your cool/hit the ceiling

11. Family Hits the Road with a Horse, a Wagon, and a Dream

page 70: 5) a. leg (2)   b. ordinary (6)   c. dream (4)   d. tape (1)   e. the road (5)   f. down (7)
g. a good start (3)

page 71: 8) See Appendix B, page 103.

page 71: 9) a. of, dream, leg   b. the road, down   c. good start, up

page 73: 12) 1. dreaming of   2. hit the road   3. out of the ordinary   4. run into   5. on the road
6. keep up with   7. settle down

12. A One-of-a-Kind Hotel

page 76: 5) a. kind (6)   b. of tea (1)   c. treatment (4)   d. a ball (7)   e. by (2)   f. the nose (5)   g. in (3)

page 77: 8) See Appendix B, page 103.

page 77: 9) a. the nose, of tea   b. carpet treatment, in, up   c. off, off

page 79: 12) 1. check in   2. wake...up   3. at all times   4. Go by
5. give you the red-carpet treatment   6. have a ball   7. not my cup of tea

13. Cyber-Romance Leads to Cross-Cultural Marriage

page 82: 5) a. in common (5)   b. boat (6)   c. lines (8)   d. long (3)   e. ages (1)   f. eyes on (2)
g. edge (4)   h. thing (7)

page 83: 8) See Appendix B, page 103.

page 83: 9) a. a trip, long, edge, boat   b. in common   c. eyes, disappointed

page 85: 12) 1. have a lot in common   2. Before long   3. took ages   4. were in the same boat   5. make
a trip   6. were nervous about   7. be disappointed   8. set eyes on   9. asked for her hand

14. Solo Sailor Operates on Himself—Via E-mail

page 88: 5) a. out (7)   b. woods (4)   c. upper lip (1)   d. world (6)   e. element (2)   f. wrong (5)   g. leg (3)

page 89: 8) See Appendix B, page 103.

page 89: 9) a. middle of, element   b. about, the woods   c. letter, wrong

page 91: 12) 1. was very concerned about   2. Why in the world   3. laid out   4. in the middle of
5. go wrong   6. kept a stiff upper lip   7. out of the woods

Review: Units 8–14

page 92:   A. 1. We just tied the knot!   2. You're out of the woods now.   3. I caught you red-handed.
    4. I paid through the nose, but I love it.   5. You're out of your mind!   6. Would you like to go out Friday?   7. I can't stand this anymore. I'm going inside.   8. Stop it! You're driving me crazy.   9. I'm having a ball!   10. This is not your cup of tea!

page 93:   B. 1. the road   2. the leg   3. nuts   4. on edge   5. place   6. for

             C. 1. c   2. d   3. j   4. a   5. i   6. g   7. b   8. e   9. h   10. f

             D. 1. in   2. in   3. on   4. in   5. on   6. in   7. on   8. in   9. in   10. in

page 94:   E. 1. leg (e)   2. hand (c)   3. lip (g)   4. nose (h)   5. hand (i)   6. eyes (d)   7. mind (a)
    8. hand (b)   9. leg (f)

             F. GOOD: I'm completely in my element; I'm really flying high; I fell madly in love last night; We're really hitting it off; I'm having a ball; You're giving me the red-carpet treatment.

                BAD: I'm scared stiff; This is the last straw!; I feel like I'm going to pass out; I'm seeing red; I'm sick and tired of this; I can't stand this anymore; I'm on edge; This is driving me crazy; Everything's going wrong.

page 95:   G. 1. nuts   2. on edge   3. ceiling   4. same boat   5. cup of tea   6. world   7. flying
    8. price   9. pipe   10. the woods

page 96:   H. Answers will vary.

             I. 1. d   2. b   3. b   4. c   5. c

page 97:   J. Answers will vary.

Appendix B: Dictations

1. **Engineer Is Enthusiastic About Odd New Home** *(page 5)*

Bruce Campbell lives in a plane **instead of** a traditional house. He **paid** $100,000 **for** it. The cabin feels large because he took most of the seats out. The bathrooms, **on the other hand**, are tiny. Bruce **is enthusiastic about** his home and **points out** that it's stronger than most. He's a bachelor **at present**. He jokes that he'll buy a bigger plane if he meets his **soul mate**.

2. **Man Eats Out and Gets More Than He Ordered** *(page 11)*

When Henry Snowden **pulled into** Burger King, he was **hungry as a bear**. He got his food **as well as** a surprise—over $4,000! Henry knew he should **give** the money **back**, but he didn't do it **right off the bat**. He had to **sleep on it**. When he **went back to** Burger King with the money, he got lunch **on the house**. Henry feels good now and **has a clear conscience**.

3. **Out on a Limb** *(page 17)*

Julia Butterfly **has spent two years** living in a tree. She**'s taking a stand** to save the redwood trees in California. She stays in the tree **around the clock** and **puts up with** many dangers and difficulties. She **looks forward to taking a** hot **shower** when she comes down. Julia has really **gone out on a limb** for her beliefs.

4. **On Top of the World** *(page 23)*

Tom had a difficult life after his car accident, but her refused to **give up** his dream. He **set his sights on** climbing Mt. Everest and **breaking new ground** as a disabled person. **Year in and year out** for ten years, he trained hard. He **made two attempts to** climb the mountain, but bad weather and illness **forced** him **back**. Finally, in 1998, he **made history.**

5. **Boy Fights Lion Tooth and Nail** *(page 29)*

When Aaron **set out on** a hike one summer day, he didn't know that he would become a hero. He was walking **in front of** Dante. He turned around when he heard a scream and **got the shock of his life**. A lion had Dante by the neck. Aaron reacted **in a flash** and **fought the lion tooth and nail**. The lion finally **let go of** Dante and **backed off**. It was **a close call**!

6. **Face-to-Face After 56 Years** *(page 35)*

Anna **gave birth to** her daughter Ludmilla during World War II. She lost her in a labor camp a year later. Anna **lived through** the war and **searched for** Ludmilla but couldn't find her. She moved to the U.S. but couldn't stop **thinking about** her daughter. Finally, Anna **found out** that Ludmilla was alive in Russia. They **made plans for** a reunion, and after 56 years, they met **face-to-face**.

7. **Globe-Trotting Frog Comes Home** *(page 41)*

The Knights first thought some kids **ripped off** their frog. But then they **heard from** the frog in New York. He said he had to **get away** but would **be back** by Christmas. **Sure enough**, after visiting many countries, the **globe-trotting** frog arrived home. The Knights **don't have a clue** who took the frog, but they **were good sports** and **got a kick out of** his adventure.

8. **Emu Falls Madly in Love** *(page 53)*

When the emu **showed up** and Ed began feeding it, he **was asking for trouble.** The bird began following him **all day long** and **driving him crazy**. One day, things **went from bad to worse**. The bird ran toward Ed making mating calls. He **was scared stiff** and didn't want to **go out of** his house. Finally, the Animal Rescue Foundation **got involved** and **helped** Ed **out**.

9. Man Ties the Knot with Stranger (page 59)

David Weinlick **was sick and tired of** people asking him when he was going to **get married**. He wasn't **going out with** anyone, but he started to **get ready for** his wedding. He organized a bridal contest to **take place** on June 13. About 25 women showed up and David married the winner. He and his new bride have **hit it off** and both are happy that they **tied the knot.**

10. Graffiti Makes Him See Red (page 65)

Mike Quintana **sees red** when he sees graffiti. He **can't stand** it. He spends a lot of time trying to **get rid of** it. Recently, Quintana **caught** three teens **red-handed**. There was a fight. Quintana **got the upper hand** and called the police. When one of the teens threatened Quintana, he **hit the ceiling**. He took a can of red paint and sprayed the boys in the face. Now he **is paying the price**.

11. Family Hits the Road with a Horse, a Wagon, and a Dream (page 71)

The Grant family **hit the road** in their wagon in 1990. They **got off to a good start,** but soon they **ran into** several problems. There was a war in the Balkans. **Red tape** in China made them go into Mongolia, 1,600 kilometers **out of the way**. They had to **drive** bandits **away**. Finally, after seven years **on the road**, the family has **settled down**.

12. A One-of-a-Kind Hotel (page 77)

Jules' Lodge is a **one-of-a-kind** hotel. To **check in**, you have to scuba dive. There are big windows where you can watch the fish **go by**. A control room monitors the hotel **at all times** and **keeps** the water **out**. You'll **pay through the nose** at the hotel, but they **give you the red-carpet treatment**. You'll **have a ball** there!

13. Cyber-Romance Leads to Cross-Cultural Marriage (page 83)

After they met on the Internet, Figen and Dan realized they **had a lot in common**. Dan decided to **make a trip** to Turkey to meet Figen. He **was on edge**. Figen **was nervous about** the meeting too, but when they **set eyes on** each other, they knew it **was the real thing**. **Before long**, Dan returned to Turkey to **ask for Figen's hand.**

14. Solo Sailor Operates on Himself—Via E-mail (page 89)

On **the first leg** of the race, Viktor **was in his element.** But then his elbow became a problem. **In the middle of** a storm, he had to operate. He **kept a stiff upper lip**, following the doctor's instructions **to the letter**. Then something **went wrong**. Blood was all over the place. He e-mailed the doctor. Finally, the doctor **put two and two together** and told Viktor to stop taking aspirin. Viktor **was out of the woods**.

Appendix C: Idiom Groups

This appendix categorizes idioms and expressions in different ways to help you learn and remember.

Idioms grouped according to form

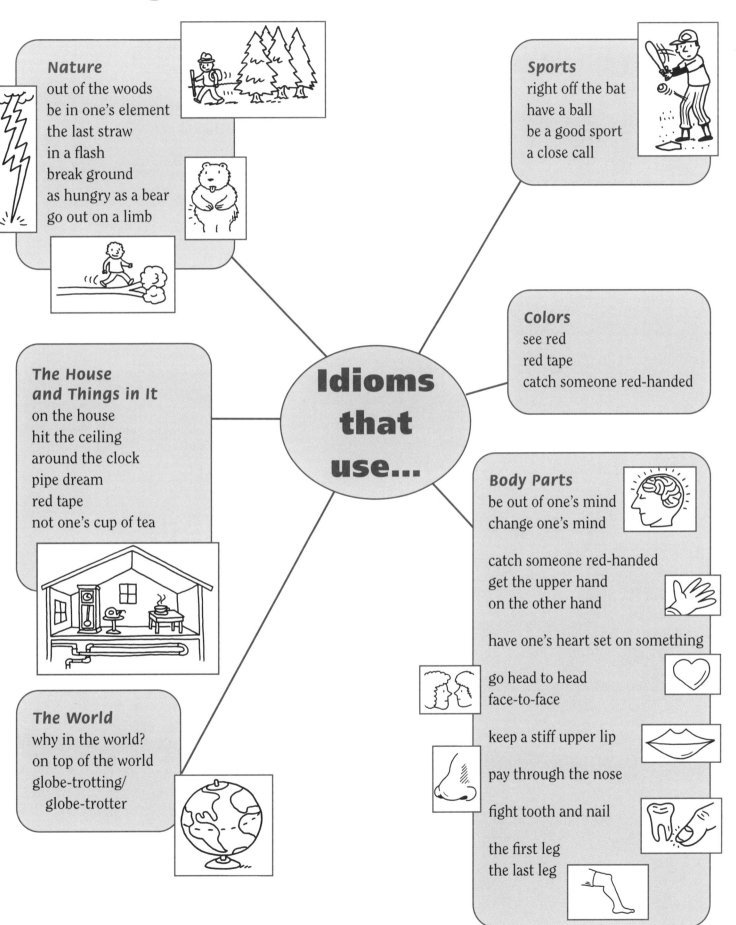

Nature
out of the woods
be in one's element
the last straw
in a flash
break ground
as hungry as a bear
go out on a limb

Sports
right off the bat
have a ball
be a good sport
a close call

The House and Things in It
on the house
hit the ceiling
around the clock
pipe dream
red tape
not one's cup of tea

Idioms that use...

Colors
see red
red tape
catch someone red-handed

Body Parts
be out of one's mind
change one's mind

catch someone red-handed
get the upper hand
on the other hand

have one's heart set on something

go head to head
face-to-face

keep a stiff upper lip

pay through the nose

fight tooth and nail

the first leg
the last leg

The World
why in the world?
on top of the world
globe-trotting/
   globe-trotter

Idioms grouped according to form

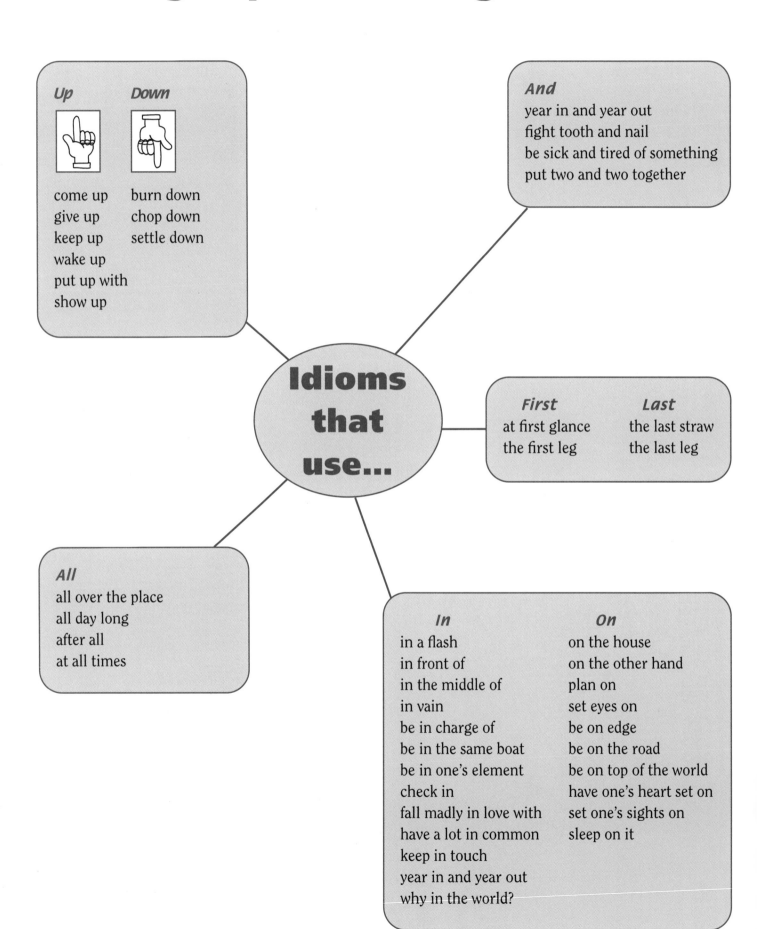

Up **Down**

come up   burn down
give up   chop down
keep up   settle down
wake up
put up with
show up

And
year in and year out
fight tooth and nail
be sick and tired of something
put two and two together

Idioms that use...

First   **Last**
at first glance   the last straw
the first leg   the last leg

All
all over the place
all day long
after all
at all times

In   **On**
in a flash   on the house
in front of   on the other hand
in the middle of   plan on
in vain   set eyes on
be in charge of   be on edge
be in the same boat   be on the road
be in one's element   be on top of the world
check in   have one's heart set on
fall madly in love with   set one's sights on
have a lot in common   sleep on it
keep in touch
year in and year out
why in the world?

Idioms grouped according to form

Idioms that use verbs

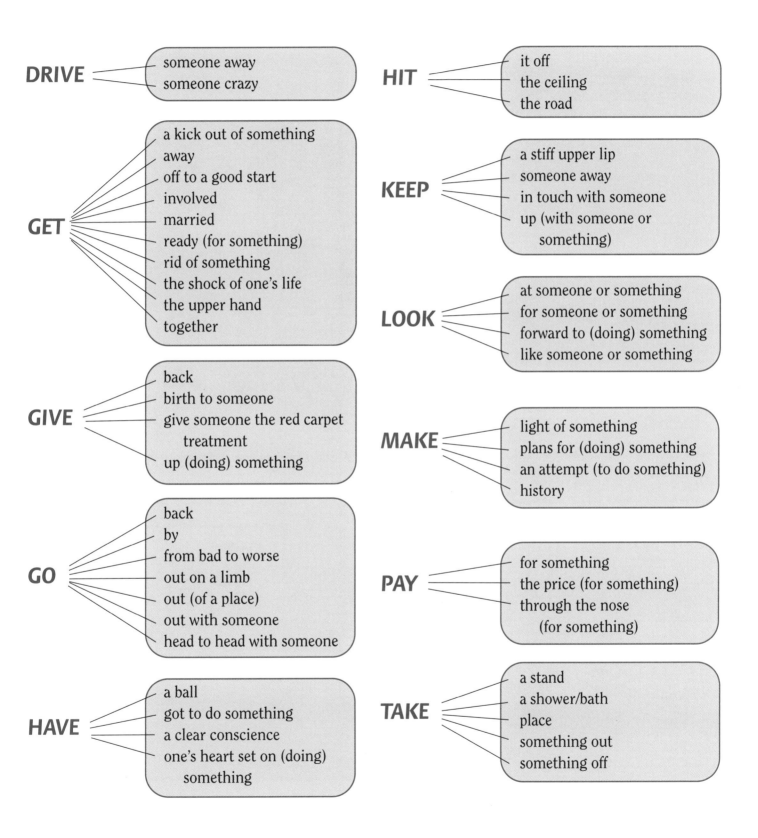

DRIVE
- someone away
- someone crazy

GET
- a kick out of something
- away
- off to a good start
- involved
- married
- ready (for something)
- rid of something
- the shock of one's life
- the upper hand
- together

GIVE
- back
- birth to someone
- give someone the red carpet treatment
- up (doing) something

GO
- back
- by
- from bad to worse
- out on a limb
- out (of a place)
- out with someone
- head to head with someone

HAVE
- a ball
- got to do something
- a clear conscience
- one's heart set on (doing) something

HIT
- it off
- the ceiling
- the road

KEEP
- a stiff upper lip
- someone away
- in touch with someone
- up (with someone or something)

LOOK
- at someone or something
- for someone or something
- forward to (doing) something
- like someone or something

MAKE
- light of something
- plans for (doing) something
- an attempt (to do something)
- history

PAY
- for something
- the price (for something)
- through the nose (for something)

TAKE
- a stand
- a shower/bath
- place
- something out
- something off

Idioms grouped according to meaning

Love and marriage

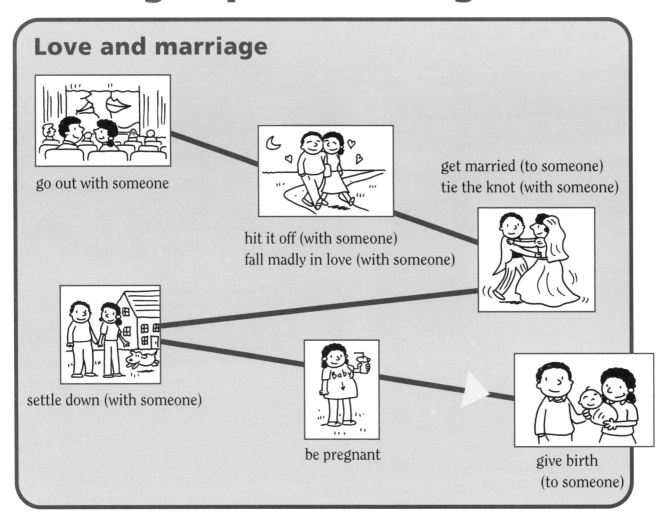

go out with someone

hit it off (with someone)
fall madly in love (with someone)

get married (to someone)
tie the knot (with someone)

settle down (with someone)

be pregnant

give birth
(to someone)

The Future

plan on (doing) something
make plans for (doing) something
get ready for something
look forward to (doing) something
have one's heart set on (doing) something
set one's sights on (doing) something
dream of (doing) something
it's a pipe dream

Idioms grouped according to meaning

Contact and communication

Verbs

keep in touch with someone
drop someone a line
hear from someone
get together (with someone)
run into someone

drive someone away
keep someone away
force someone back
back off

Adverb
face-to-face

Travel

Verbs

Starting the trip
set out (on a trip)
hit the road
get off to a good start

Taking the trip
be on the road
check in (to a hotel)
eat out

Ending the trip
go back
be back

Nouns
the first leg (of the trip)
the last leg (of the trip)

Adjective
globe-trotting

Adverb
out of the way

Idioms grouped according to meaning

Time

continuously:	all day long, around the clock, at all times, year after year, year in and year out
now:	at present
immediately:	right off the bat, at first glance
soon:	before long
very quickly:	in a flash
during:	in the middle of something

Feeling good

be flying high
be on top of the world
be in one's element
be enthusiastic about something
get a kick out of something
have a ball

fall madly in love with someone
hit it off with someone

have a clear conscience

Feeling bad

be sick of something
be sick and tired of something
can't stand something

Anger
lose one's cool
hit the ceiling
see red

Fear
be scared (of something)
be scared stiff (of something)

Shock
get the shock of one's life

Concern
be concerned about someone
or something

Sickness
pass out

Appendix D: Phrasal Verbs

I. What is *a phrasal verb?*

A phrasal verb is a verb + a particle.

> *I wonder when Luisa will **show up.***
> (verb)(particle)
>
> *The thief **ripped** me **off**.*
> (verb)   (particle)

In English, many phrasal verbs are idiomatic; you cannot understand the meaning of the whole from the parts. *Show up* means "arrive," and *rip off* means "steal."

II. Phrasal verbs fall into different categories.

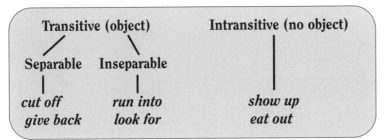

a. Some phrasal verbs are *transitive*; others are *intransitive*.

Transitive phrasal verbs take a direct object.

> *I **cut off** <u>my hair</u>.*   *I **ran into** <u>Sylvia</u> today.*
> *He **gave back** <u>my bike</u>.*   *I'm **looking for** <u>my cat</u>.*

Intransitive phrasal verbs do not take an object.

> *Jaime plans to come but isn't sure when he'll **show up**.*
> *Do you want to **eat out**?*

b. Some transitive phrasal verbs are *separable* (that is, the object can come between the two parts of the verb); others are *inseparable*.

Separable phrasal verbs	Inseparable phrasal verbs
<u>**help out**</u> *I **helped out** my neighbor.* *I **helped** my neighbor **out**.* *I **helped** her **out**.*	<u>**run into**</u> *I **ran into** Sylvia today.* *I **ran into** her today.*
<u>**give back**</u> *He **gave back** my bike.* *He **gave** my bike **back**.* *He **gave** it **back**.*	<u>**look for**</u> *I'm **looking for** my cat.* *I'm **looking for** it.*

When a phrasal verb is **separable**, you can put a noun either between the verb and the particle or after the particle. If you use a pronoun *(he, she, it, me, we, you, they)*, the pronoun <u>must</u> go between the verb and the particle. If a phrasal verb is **inseparable**, the noun and pronoun always come after the particle.

III. Phrasal verbs from this book

BACK OFF (intransitive): move in reverse; stop threatening
*The angry dog made us **back off**.*

BACK OFF FROM (transitive, inseparable): move in reverse; stop threatening someone or something
*Duane didn't want to fight, so he **backed off from** Pietro.*

BELONG TO (transitive, inseparable): be the property of someone
*That bike is not mine; it **belongs to** Fernando.*
*That bike is not mine; it **belongs to** him.*

BURN DOWN (transitive, separable): destroy something by fire
*The man carelessly tossed his cigarette and **burned down** the shed.*
*The man carelessly tossed his cigarette and **burned** the shed **down**.*
*The man carelessly tossed his cigarette and **burned** it **down**.*

CHECK IN (intransitive): register at a hotel, a convention, a hospital, etc.
*When I arrived at the conference last night, I immediately **checked in**.*

CHOP DOWN (transitive, separable): cut something down, usually a tree
*Let's **chop down** the tree. It's dead!*
*Let's **chop** the tree **down**. It's dead!*
*Let's **chop** it **down**. It's dead!*

COME UP (intransitive): rise (referring to the sun, moon, etc.)
*I always get up when the sun **comes up**.*

DO AWAY WITH (transitive, inseparable): put an end to; destroy something
*The mayor is trying to **do away with** drugs.*
*The mayor is trying to **do away with** them.*

DREAM OF (transitive, inseparable): think about something that you wish for the future
*Do you **dream of** being a basketball star?*
*Do you often **dream of** it?*

DRIVE AWAY (transitive, separable): force someone to leave
*The bad smells outside the restaurant **drove away** customers.*
*The bad smells outside the restaurant **drove** customers **away**.*
*The bad smells outside the restaurant **drove** them **away**.*

DRY OFF (intransitive): become dry
*I'd like to sit in the sun and **dry off**.*

EAT OUT (intransitive): eat in a restaurant
*Hilda hates to cook, so she often **eats out**.*

FIND OUT (transitive, separable): learn or discover something
*Did you **find out** their plan?*
*Did you **find** it **out**?*
Note: This verb is only separated when *it* is used.

FORCE BACK (transitive, separable): make someone go back
*The bad weather **forced back** the mountaineers.*
*The bad weather **forced** the mountaineers **back**.*
*The bad weather **forced** them **back**.*

GET AWAY (intransitive): leave one's daily routine; go on vacation
*Maria has worked hard for the last six months and needs to **get away**.*

GIVE BACK (transitive, separable): return something (to someone)
*Please **give back** my pencil.*
*Please **give** my pencil **back**.*
*Please **give** it **back**.*

GIVE UP (transitive, separable): stop or quit (doing) something
*She should **give up** smoking.*
*She should **give** smoking **up**.*
*She should **give** it **up**.*

GO BACK (intransitive): return
*Marissa loved her trip to Mexico; she wants to **go back**.*

GO BACK TO (transitive, inseparable): return to a place
*Marissa wants to **go back to** Mexico.*
Note: We usually don't say *go back to it,* but rather *go back there.*

GO BY (intransitive): pass; move past
*Let's watch the parade **go by**.*

GO BY (transitive, inseparable): pass; move past someone or something
*Let's **go by** the library on the way home.*
*Let's **go by** it on the way home.*

GO OUT (intransitive): leave
*It was very late when I **went out**.*

GO OUT OF (transitive, inseparable): leave a place
*When I **went out of** the movie theater, I was still laughing.*

GO OUT WITH (transitive, inseparable): go somewhere with a friend; have a romance with someone
*Joseph would like to **go out with** Ludmilla on Saturday night.*
*Josh would like to **go out with** Lilly.*

HAND OUT (transitive, separable): distribute something
*They're **handing out** free cookies over there.*
*They're **handing** free cookies **out** over there.*
*They're **handing** them **out** over there.*

HEAR FROM (transitive, inseparable): receive a phone call, letter, or e-mail from someone
*I **heard from** my brother in China last week.*
*I **heard from** him last week.*

HELP OUT (intransitive): be helpful
*I see you're very busy. Please let me know if I can **help out**.*

HELP OUT (transitive, separable): be helpful to someone
*I **helped out** my cousin when she needed money.*
*I **helped** my cousin **out** when she needed money.*
*I **helped** her **out** when she needed money.*

KEEP AWAY (transitive, separable): make someone or something stay at a distance
*Please **keep away** that dog.*
*Please **keep** that dog **away**.*
*Please **keep** it **away**.*

KEEP OUT (transitive, separable): not allow someone or something to enter
*We like to close the door to **keep out** the mosquitoes.*
*We need to **keep** the mosquitoes **out**.*
*We need to **keep** them **out**.*

KEEP UP (intransitive): maintain the pace
*You walk so fast; it's hard to **keep up**!*

KEEP UP WITH (transitive, inseparable): maintain the pace of someone or something
*It's hard to **keep up with** fashion; it changes so fast.*
*It's hard to **keep up with** it; it changes so fast.*

LAY OUT (transitive, separable): arrange; organize something
*Before I pack, I'll **lay out** my clothes on the bed.*
*Before I pack, I'll **lay** my clothes **out** on the bed.*
*Before I pack, I'll **lay** them **out** on the bed.*

LET GO OF (transitive, inseparable): release someone or something
*Please **let go of** my arm.*
*Please **let go of** it.*

LIVE THROUGH (transitive, inseparable): survive something
*Herve didn't think he would **live through** the hurricane.*
*Herve didn't think he would **live through** it.*

LOOK AT (transitive, inseparable): direct your eyes to someone or something
***Look at** the balloon in the sky!*
***Look at** it!*

LOOK FOR (transitive, inseparable): try to find someone or something
*I **looked for** the cat, but he was gone!*
*I **looked for** him, but he was gone!*
Note: The verb can only be separated by an adverb, not an object:
*I **looked** everywhere **for** the cat, but he was gone!*
*I **looked** everywhere **for** him, but he was gone!*

LOOK FORWARD TO (transitive, inseparable): anticipate (doing) something with pleasure
*I always **look forward to** my birthday.*
*I always **look forward to** it.*

PASS OUT (intransitive): lose consciousness; faint
*The sun was so hot that I almost **passed out**.*

PAY FOR (transitive, inseparable): give money for something
*I **paid for** the gas.*
*I **paid for** it.*
Note: The verb can only be separated by a phrase that tells how much:
*I **paid** a lot **for** the gas.*
*I **paid** $25.00 **for** it.*

PLAN ON (transitive, inseparable): expect (to do) something in the future
*I didn't **plan on** a big party, but 50 people came.*
*I didn't **plan on** it, but 50 people came.*

POINT OUT (transitive, separable): explain something; show something
*Our nature guide **pointed out** the many flowers to us.*
*Our nature guide **pointed** the many flowers **out** to us.*
*Our nature guide **pointed** them **out** to us.*

PULL INTO (transitive, inseparable): arrive at a place by car, bus, or train
*Tonia **pulled into** the parking lot and turned off the car.*
*Tonia **pulled into** it and turned off the car.*

PUT UP WITH (transitive, inseparable): endure or tolerate someone or something
*He doesn't **put up with** dishonesty.*
*He doesn't **put up with** it.*

RIP OFF (transitive, separable): steal something; steal from someone
*The **thief ripped off** my car.*
*The **thief ripped** my car **off**.*
*The **thief ripped** it **off**.*

RUN INTO (transitive, inseparable): meet someone or something unexpectedly
*I **ran into** my aunt at the supermarket.*
*I **ran into** her at the supermarket.*

SEARCH FOR (transitive, inseparable): look everywhere for someone or something
*Nina **searched for** her diamond ring.*
*Nina **searched for** it.*
Note: The verb can only be separated by an adverb, not by an object:
*Nina **searched** everywhere **for** her diamond ring.*
*Nina **searched** everywhere **for** it.*

SET OUT (intransitive): begin a hike, a walk, a trip, an adventure, etc.
*What time are you planning to **set out**?*

SET OUT ON (transitive, inseparable): begin a hike, a walk, a trip, an adventure, etc.
*We're going to **set out on** our hike at 2 P.M.*

SETTLE DOWN (intransitive): begin to live a stable life in one place
*At age 40, Natasha finally decided to get married and **settle down**.*

SHOW UP (intransitive): arrive somewhere; appear
*The party starts at 9 P.M. What time will you **show up**?*

TAKE OFF (transitive, separable): remove clothing, jewelry, makeup, a cover from a jar, etc.
*Do you want to **take off** your coat?*
*Do you want to **take** your coat **off**?*
*Do you want to **take** it **off**?*

TAKE OUT (transitive, separable): remove something
*Igor **took out** the garbage.*
*Igor **took** the garbage **out**.*
*Igor **took** it **out**.*

THINK ABOUT (transitive, inseparable): remember; consider someone or something
*I often **think about** leaving this crazy city.*
*I often **think about** it.*

WAKE UP (intransitive): awaken from sleep
*It's always hard for me to **wake up**.*

WAKE UP (transitive, separable): awaken someone from sleep
*Quiet! Don't **wake up** the baby!*
*Quiet! Don't **wake** the baby **up**!*
*Quiet! Don't **wake** her **up**!*

Idiom and Definition	Usage	Example	Language notes	Similar expressions	Opposite expressions
a bitter pill to swallow (4) a difficult thing to accept		When Fernando's fiancee broke their engagement, it was a bitter pill for him to swallow.	You can insert *for someone* in this expression, as in the example. The expression is usually used with the verb *be*.	hard to swallow (informal) hard to take	
a close call (5) a narrow escape		My car almost hit that tree. What a close call!	Used as in the example, or with *be* or *have*: *I had a close call; It was a close call.*	a near miss have a brush with something a close shave (informal)	
a dream come true (6) a dream that has become a reality		When Larissa met Jose, he seemed like a dream come true!			a pipe dream one's worst nightmare
a pipe dream (11) an unrealistic plan		Jorge wants to build a large house, but it's a pipedream. He has no money and no job!	This is a noun phrase, usually used with the verb *be,* as in the example.	a daydream an idle fancy pie in the sky (informal)	a dream come true
according to someone or something (3) as said by someone or something		According to the weather report, it's going to rain today.	Do not use *me* after *according to*. Instead, say *in my opinion.*	in the words of someone by all accounts	
after all (8) one must remember that; consider the fact that		David should listen to his mother; after all, she knows what is best for him.	The stress in this expression is on *all*. When the stress is on *after,* the expression means *anyway,* as in *Bob didn't want to go, but he went after all.*	all things considered after all is said and done bear in mind	

Idiom and Definition	Usage	Example	Language notes	Similar expressions	Opposite expressions
all day long (8) during the entire day		Masaya works the night shift and then sleeps all day long.	The word *long* emphasizes the continuous nature of an activity. You can also say *all week long, all month long, all year long.*	around the clock twenty-four hours a day all the time	all night long
all over the place (10, 14) everywhere		His house is a mess. There are papers and clothes all over the place.		here, there, and everywhere (informal) all over creation (informal)	in one spot here and there (= in a few places)
around the clock (3) continuously; without a break		CNN broadcasts news around the clock.	This expression can also form an adjective, as in *CNN has around-the-clock news* (= continuous news). Note that the adjective form uses hyphens.	all the time at all times 24 hours a day non-stop	from time to time once in a while at intervals
(as) hungry as a bear (2) very hungry	informal	I haven't eaten in 24 hours and I'm as hungry as a bear.	The first *as* is optional. An expression similar to the example is *I'm so hungry I could eat a horse.*	eat like a horse/pig dying of hunger	be full be stuffed (informal)

Idiom and Definition	Usage	Example	Language notes	Similar expressions	Opposite expressions
as well as (2) and also		I enjoy tennis as well as golf.	*As well as* is used in the middle of a sentence to connect two things. *As well* can also appear at the end of a sentence: *I enjoy tennis and golf as well.*	in addition to	
ask for someone's hand (13) ask for permission to marry someone	formal	Sandra was happy when Alex got down on his knees and asked for her hand.		ask for someone's hand in marriage (formal) pop the question (informal)	break up (with someone) split up (with someone)
ask for trouble (8) do something that will cause problems later	informal	If you keep a gun in the house with young children, you are asking for trouble.		play with fire (informal) skate on thin ice (informal) stretch one's luck (informal) tempt fate play Russian roulettte	play it safe stay out of harm's reach be on the safe side look before you leap (informal)
at all times (12) constantly; continuously		Luis carries his cellular phone at all times so that he won't miss an important call.		all the time around the clock twenty-four hours a day	off and on once in a while every so often at intervals once in a blue moon (informal)
at first glance (5) at the first quick look		At first glance, I thought my hand was bleeding, but then I realized it was just red ink from my pen.		at first at first blush	in the end
at present (1) now		I'm busy at present; can I call you later?	This expression is short for *at the present time.*	right now at this point in time at the present time	in the future later on in a while

Idiom and Definition	Usage	Example	Language notes	Similar expressions	Opposite expressions
back off (from someone)(5) move in reverse; stop threatening (someone)		I thought Igor and Pierre were going to fight, but Igor backed off.	*Back off* is intransitive. *Back off from* is transitive and inseparable. *Back off* also means *yield* in an argument. Don't confuse *back off* with *back up,* which means *go in reverse in your car.*	back away beat a retreat	come at someone
be a good sport (7) be able to laugh at jokes and pranks that involve you	informal	We laugh at Tom when he dances, but he's a good sport and just laughs with us.		have a good attitude take things in stride play along with someone or something have a good sense of humor	be a sore loser be a poor loser have no sense of humor be a sourpuss (informal)
be back (7) be again where you were before		I'm going to school now, but I'll be back at 5:00.		go back	be gone be away be on vacation
be concerned about someone or something (14) worry about someone or something		Mary just lost her job, and she's concerned about money.		be worried (about someone or something) lose sleep over something (informal)	be unconcerned about someone or something not give a darn/a damn about someone or something (slang)
be disappointed by someone or something (13) feel that your hopes were not met by someone or something		I was disappointed by my history class because the teacher was boring.	You can also be disappointed *in* someone or something.	be let down by someone or something have one's hopes dashed by someone or something	be satisfied with someone or something

Idiom and Definition	Usage	Example	Language notes	Similar expressions	Opposite expressions
be enthusiastic about something (1) like something very much		Jack is enthusiastic about fishing because he loves eating fish!	*Be enthusiastic about* can be followed by a noun or a gerund (verb + *ing*).	be pumped about something (informal) be fired up about something (informal) be (all) charged up about something (informal) be nuts/wild/crazy about something (informal) be gung-ho about something (slang)	be indifferent toward/about something be blasé about something (informal) be lukewarm about something (informal) not give a darn/a damn about something (slang)
be flying high (9) be very happy	informal	Naomi was flying high after she won the lottery; she kept dancing around the room and kissing everyone.		be beside oneself (with joy) be in high spirits be on top of the world (informal) be in seventh heaven (informal) be on cloud nine (informal)	be in low spirits be down in the dumps (informal) be down at the mouth (informal)
be in charge (of someone or something) (5, 14) be responsible (for someone or something)		You should talk to my boss. He's in charge of the project.	You can also *be in charge of doing something*, as in *I'm in charge of paying the bills.*	be in command (of someone or something) be at the helm (of something) be at the head (of something) be in the saddle (informal) be head honcho (slang)	work for someone play second fiddle to someone (informal) be an underling (informal)

Idiom and Definition	Usage	Example	Language notes	Similar expressions	Opposite expressions
be in one's element (14) be in a happy and comfortable situation		Ahmed, who loves books, is in his element at the library.		be/feel at home feel at ease	be out of one's element be a fish out of water be a square peg in a round hole
be in the same boat (as someone) (13) be in the same situation, with the same problem(s)	informal	The two strangers missed the last train. Realizing they were both in the same boat, they shared a taxi into town.		be in the same fix (informal) be in the same pickle (informal) be in the same tight spot (informal)	
be nervous about something (13) feel afraid and a little excited about something		Mehmet thinks he will do well at his new job, but he's nervous about meeting all the new people.		be concerned about something be in a stew about something (informal) have butterflies in one's stomach (informal)	be calm about something be (as) cool as a cucumber (informal) be laid-back about something (informal)
be nuts (13) be crazy; insane	informal	Many people think Leyla is nuts for leaving her important job at the university to live in a cabin in the woods.	You can also *go nuts,* which means *become crazy.*	be crazy; be bananas; be nutty as a fruitcake (informal) have a screw loose (informal) be stark raving mad (informal) be out of one's mind (informal)	be clear-headed be of sound mind
be on edge (13) be nervous		As a tourist in New York City, Mimi was on edge. She had heard so many stories of crime!		be jittery (informal) be in a tizzy (slang) be in a stew (slang)	be at ease be laid-back (informal) be (as) cool as a cucumber (informal) keep one's cool (informal)

Idiom and Definition	Usage	Example	Language notes	Similar expressions	Opposite expressions
be on top of the world (4) be very happy	informal	When Lorenzo was named president of the company, he was on top of the world.		be on cloud nine (informal) be in seventh heaven (informal) be flying high (informal) be walking on air (informal) be beside oneself (with joy) (informal)	be/feel blue have a heavy heart be down (informal) be down in the dumps (informal) be down at the mouth (informal)
be out of one's mind (9) be crazy, irrational, silly	informal	You're out of your mind to try something as dangerous as sky-diving!	You can also *go out of your mind,* which means *become crazy* or *silly.*	be crazy/nuts/ bananas (informal) have a screw loose (informal) be nutty as a fruitcake (informal) be off one's rocker (informal)	be of sound mind be in one's right mind (informal)
be out of the woods (14) be out of danger after an illness, injury, or very difficult situation	informal	After Brenda's heart attack, she was in the hospital on life support for weeks, but she gradually improved and is now out of the woods.		pull through (an illness) be out of harm's way be on the road to recovery be home free (informal)	be in danger be on thin ice (informal) be hanging by a thread (informal) have one foot in the grave (informal)
be pregnant (6) be going to have a baby		Seiko is pregnant with her first child and is trying to choose a name for the baby.	You can *be five months pregnant, be six months pregnant,* etc.	be expecting (informal) be 3 (4, 5, etc.) months along (informal) be in the family way (informal) have a cake/a loaf in the oven (slang)	

Idiom and Definition	Usage	Example	Language notes	Similar expressions	Opposite expressions
be scared of someone or something (5) fear; be afraid of someone or something		I won't swim in the ocean because I'm scared of sharks.	You can also *be scared of doing something.*	be frightened of someone or something be afraid of someone or something be scared to death of someone or something (informal)	be fearless/ unafraid/ unintimidated
be scared stiff (of someone or something) (8) be very afraid (of someone or something)	informal	After I saw that horror film, I was scared stiff for three days!		be scared to death be out of one's wits be scared silly (informal) be petrified (informal) be white with fear be white as a sheet	be calm be (as) cool as a cucumber (informal)
be sick and tired of something (9) feel unable to tolerate something any longer	informal	Charles decided to move to sunny Florida because he's sick and tired of the long, cold winters in Chicago.	This expression is similar to, but stronger than, *be sick of something* or *be tired of something.* It can be followed by a gerund, as in *I'm sick and tired of studying.*	have all one can stand of someone or something be fed up with someone or something (informal)	be enthusiastic about something be interested in something be gung-ho about something (informal) be tickled pink about something (informal)
be sick of something (7) be tired of; be bored with something	informal	Ming was sick of the rainy weather in Seattle, so she took a trip to California.	This expression can be followed by a gerund (verb + *ing*), as in *I'm sick of cooking. Let's go out to eat!*	be fed up with something (informal) be bored stiff with something (informal)	be interested in someone or something be enchanted by someone or something

Idiom and Definition	Usage	Example	Language notes	Similar expressions	Opposite expressions
be the real thing (13) be genuine and authentic	informal	The jeweler examined Ludmilla's ring and said the diamond was the real thing.		be the genuine article (informal) be the real McCoy (informal)	be a fake be a phoney (informal) be a con artist (said of a person)
before long (13) in a short time; soon		Mother Earth will be destroyed before long if we don't take care of the environment.		in a while in the near future in a little while (informal)	
belong to someone (1) be the property of someone		I found this book in my car. Does it belong to you?	Phrasal verb (trans, insep) The example could also read *I found this book in my car. Is it yours?*		
break new ground (4) do something that has not been done before		Alexander Graham Bell broke new ground when he invented the telephone.	You can break new ground *in something* or *by doing something.* Don't confuse this expression with *break ground for something,* which means start digging the foundation for a new building.	be on the cutting edge (of something) be in the vanguard (of something) be avant-garde blaze a (new) trail	re-invent the wheel go over old ground be behind the times
burn something down (6) destroy something by fire		He fell asleep with a lighted cigarette and burned his house down.	Phrasal verb (trans, sep)	burn something to the ground set fire to something reduce something to ashes	put a fire out
by mistake (2) accidentally; in error		Hideaki got on the wrong train by mistake and went to Boston instead of Washington, D.C.		by accident by a fluke	on purpose by choice by design with one's eyes wide open

Idiom and Definition	Usage	Example	Language notes	Similar expressions	Opposite expressions
can't stand something (10) dislike something very much	informal	When I was younger I liked to exercise, but now I can't stand it!	Sometimes the expression is expanded to *can't stand the sight/smell/sound/ thought of something.*	can't bear something can't stomach something have no use for something	be crazy/wild/nuts about something (informal) be into something (informal) love something to pieces (informal)
catch someone red-handed (10) catch someone in the act of doing something wrong		Amy's brother tried to steal a CD player from the department store, but a security guard caught him red-handed.	The expression is often used in the passive voice, as in *He was caught red-handed.*	catch someone in the act	turn a blind eye (to someone's crime) be hoodwinked (by someone) (informal) get away scot-free (informal)
change one's mind (7) change one's opinion or point of view		I was going to buy a car, but I changed my mind. I bought a motorcycle instead.	Note the plural forms: *They changed their minds; We changed our minds.* *Change someone's mind* means *cause a person to think differently about something.*	have second thoughts (about something) do an about-face change one's tune (informal) sing a different tune (informal)	make up one's mind (=decide for sure) be pigheaded/be as stubborn as a mule (informal = unwilling to change one's mind)
check in (12) register at a hotel, a convention, a hospital, etc.		The hotel clerk asked for Tahira's passport when she checked in.	Phrasal verb (intrans) The phrasal verb *check into* is transitive and inseparable: *He checked into the hospital.*	sign in	check out sign out
chop something down (3) cut something down, usually a tree		The trees in the park have Dutch Elm disease, so the city is going to to chop them down.	Phrasal verb (trans, sep)	cut something down	

Idiom and Definition	Usage	Example	Language notes	Similar expressions	Opposite expressions
come up (4) rise (referring to the sun, moon, etc.)		The sun will come up at 6:20 tomorrow morning.	Phrasal verb (intrans)	come over the horizon	go down
do away with something (10) put an end to something; destroy something		Lupe chose to study economics in college because her dream was to do away with poverty.	Phrasal verb (trans, insep)	get rid of something put an end to something dispose of something	bring something forth give birth (to something)
dream of (doing) something (11) think about (doing) something that you wish for the future		Arturo does not like working for other people and dreams of having his own business someday.	Phrasal verb (trans, insep)	harbor the idea of doing something	give up on one's dreams
drive someone away (11) force someone to leave		Paul is so loud and rude that he drives people away.	Phrasal verb (trans, sep)	force someone out (of a place)	draw someone toward you
drive someone crazy (8) annoy or irritate someone	informal	Children who scream and shout drive me crazy.		make someone crazy try someone's patience drive someone mad (informal) drive someone up the wall (informal) grate on someone's nerves (informal)	set someone at ease

Idiom and Definition	Usage	Example	Language notes	Similar expressions	Opposite expressions
drop someone a line (7) write a short letter to someone	informal	I haven't heard from Yilmaz in a year; I should drop him a line.		drop someone a note get in touch with someone	
dry off (12) become dry		After the river rafting trip, I was completely wet; so I sat in the sun and dried off.	Phrasal verb (intrans) *Dry something off* is transitive and separable and means *make something dry*. *Dry up* also means *become dry,* but it is used in the sense of *evaporate,* as in *It was so hot that the lake dried up.*		get wet
eat out (2) eat in a restaurant		I don't like restaurant food, so I never eat out.	Phrasal verb (intrans)	go out to eat dine out go out for a bite to eat	eat in
face-to-face (6) in direct contact; in person		It was nice to meet Monika face-to-face after years of e-mailing.	The expression is often used with the verbs *meet, stand,* and *sit.*	in person nose to nose eyeball to eyeball	
fall madly in love (with someone) (8, 13) begin to love (someone) very much	informal	When Hans saw Maria at the dance, he thought she looked like an angel and fell madly in love with her.		fall head over heels in love (with someone) (informal) fall for someone (informal) be swept off one's feet by someone (informal)	fall out of love (with someone)

Idiom and Definition	Usage	Example	Language notes	Similar expressions	Opposite expressions
fight tooth and nail (5) fight very hard	informal	The dogs were fighting tooth and nail and were completely bloody.	The expression can also be used when physical force is not involved: *The mayor fought the new law tooth and nail.*	fight it out slug it out go at it tooth and nail (informal) fight like devils (informal)	get along (with someone) kiss and make up
find something out (6) learn or discover something		When Elena did some research on her family tree, she found out that her grandfather had been in prison. She found that out when she did research on her family tree.	Phrasal verb (trans, sep) *Find out* can be separable, but usually only the word *it* or *that* separates the two parts of the verb. More commonly, the object is placed after *find out*, e.g., *I found out the truth, I found out that he lied,* etc. Often the expression is followed by *who, how, when, that,* and *about,* as in *I found out who was responsible* or *I just found out about the test.*	come to know something get wind of something become aware of something	be blind to something be deaf to something not have the foggiest idea/notion about something (informal)
follow the crowd (1) do what everyone else does		Norbert wants a tattoo because his friends have them; he always follows the crowd.		jump/get on the bandwagon swim with the tide follow the fashion	stand apart swim against the tide/current march to the tune of a different drummer (informal)
force someone back (4) make someone go back		The lion tamer at the circus forced back the lions with his whip. The lion tamer at the circus forced the lions back with his whip.	Phrasal verb (trans, sep)	drive someone back push someone back make someone retrace their steps	

Idiom and Definition	Usage	Example	Language notes	Similar expressions	Opposite expressions
get a kick out of something (7) enjoy something a lot	informal	Tom's old photos of us were so funny. I really got a kick out of them!		get a charge out of something (informal) get a bang out of something (informal) delight in something	be bored (stiff) with something
get away (7) leave one's daily routine; go on vacation		I've had such a busy schedule at the office this year; I really need to get away!	Phrasal verb (intrans) This expression can be followed by *from,* as in *I'd like to get away from work for a week. Get away* also means *escape.*	take a break take a vacation	stay put
get involved (with something) (8) become active or interested (in something)		Hassan just started graduate school and is getting very involved with his studies.	*Get involved with someone* means *begin a romantic relationship with someone.* Note that *get involved in something* has a similar meaning, namely, *become very interested in what you are doing.*	be involved (with something) participate in something take part (in something)	distance oneself from something steer clear of something wash one's hands of something
get married (to someone) (9) marry (someone)		Perry and Alice plan to get married after they finish college.	After you *get married,* you *are married.*	tie the knot (with someone) get hitched (slang)	get a divorce (from someone) get divorced (from someone) split up (informal)

LEXICON

Idiom and Definition	Usage	Example	Language notes	Similar expressions	Opposite expressions
get off to a good start (11) have a successful beginning		Terry's new restaurant got off to a good start when the local newspaper printed a very favorable review.		get off to a flying start (informal)	get off to a bad start start on the wrong foot (informal)
get ready (for something) (9) prepare (for something)		Greta is getting ready for her solo camping trip very carefully; if she forgets something, it could be dangerous.	You can also *get ready to do something,* as in *Greta is getting ready to take a trip.*	get set (for something)	wing it (informal, =do something with no preparation)
get rid of something (10) remove; throw something away		I cleaned my closet and got rid of my old clothes.	Sometimes *be* is used in this expression, as in *I'd like to be rid of that old car.*	throw something away throw something out toss something out do away with something dispose of something deep-six something (slang)	hang on to/hold on to something (=keep)
get the shock of one's life (5) be extremely surprised or scared	informal	Maria got the shock of her life when she heard the winning lottery number—it was hers!		be dumbfounded be bowled over (by something) (informal)	keep one's cool (informal) not blink an eye (informal)
get the upper hand (10) get the power or advantage		When Ricardo negotiates with his business competitors, he tries hard to get the upper hand.	You can *get the upper hand on someone,* as in *Ricardo tries to get the upper hand on his competitors.*	gain the upper hand get the edge on someone get the better of someone	lose out
get together (with someone) (6) meet and spend time (with someone)		George and Mary met on the Internet, and they hope to get together sometime in the future.	You can *get together with someone for something,* as in *I got together with Sam for dinner.*	rendez-vous	

Idiom and Definition	Usage	Example	Language notes	Similar expressions	Opposite expressions
give birth (to a baby) (6) have a baby		Last night Ana gave birth to a healthy baby boy.	*Give birth to something* means *start something new*, as in *The artist gave birth to a new kind of sculpture.*	bring a baby into the world	
give someone the red-carpet treatment (12) welcome a guest with special attention		I'm a regular customer at the Peking Palace restaurant, so they always give me the red-carpet treatment.		roll out the red carpet (for someone) welcome someone with open arms wine and dine someone put out the welcome mat (informal)	turn one's back on someone have nothing to do with someone
give something back (to someone)(2) return something (to someone)		Can you give me back my dictionary? I need it. Can you give my dictionary back to me? I need it.	Phrasal verb (trans, sep)	bring something back	get something back
give up (doing) something (4) stop or quit (doing) something		I'm going to give up studying dance; it's just too tiring.	Phrasal verb (trans, sep) *Give up* can also mean *stop trying,* in which case it is intransitive: *Don't give up! If you continue working hard, you'll succeed.*	cut out (doing) something put an end (stop) to (doing) something	keep on doing something go on doing something keep at it stick it out (informal)

Idiom and Definition	Usage	Example	Language notes	Similar expressions	Opposite expressions
globe-trotting (7) traveling around the world		Gordana is a globe-trotting musician; she has played in six countries in the past six months.	In the example, the expression is an adjective. It can also be used as a noun, as in *Jim's wife doesn't like his constant globe-trotting.* A person who travels a lot is a *globe-trotter.*		stay-at-home
go back (to a place) (2, 13) return (to a place)		After 50 years, Pavel is going back to visit the house where he was born.	Phrasal verb *Go back* is intransitive. *Go back to* is transitive and inseparable.		
go by (someone or something) (12) pass; move past (someone or something)		When I go by the library, I always stop to get a few books.	Phrasal verb (intrans or trans, insep)	pass by	
go from bad to worse (8) go from a bad situation to a very bad situation	informal	My rash is going from bad to worse. First it covered my finger, but now it's all over my hand.		get worse	get better
go head to head (with someone) (3) argue or fight (with someone)		Paco and his wife are always going head to head about how to spend their money.		be at odds (with someone) be at loggerheads (with someone) lock horns (with someone)	keep the peace kiss and make up (informal) bury the hatchet (informal, = stop fighting)

Idiom and Definition	Usage	Example	Language notes	Similar expressions	Opposite expressions
go out (of a place) (8) leave (a place)		The dog went out of the gate while we were not looking.	Phrasal verb *Go out* is intransitive. *Go out of* is transitive and inseparable. *Go out* can also mean *leave one's house for the purposes of entertainment.*	walk out (of a place)	go in (to a place) set foot in a place
go out on a limb (3) do something that could have dangerous consequences		My boss hates to spend money, but I went out on a limb anyway and asked for a raise.	A limb is a tree branch, so the expression indicates a dangerous position.	take a chance take a risk put oneself on the line risk one's neck (informal) stick one's neck out (informal) skate on thin ice (informal) play with fire (informal) rock the boat (informal) make waves (informal)	be careful play it safe (informal)
go out with someone (9) have a romance with someone; go somewhere with a friend		Bill went out with Carrie for two years before they got engaged. Do you want to go out and see a movie tonight?	Phrasal verb (trans, insep) Note that this expression has two different usages, as in the examples.	have a date (with someone) take someone out go steady (with someone)	break up (with someone)
go wrong (14) fail; not happen as planned		I tried to cook a nice dinner for my boss, but everything went wrong. I burned the meat and undercooked the potatoes!	The subject used with *go wrong* is usually an indefinite pronoun, such as *everything, something, nothing, many things,* etc.	go amiss turn out badly not pan out (informal) go up in smoke (informal) come to grief (informal) be a washout (slang)	pan out (informal) turn out fine

Idiom and Definition	Usage	Example	Language notes	Similar expressions	Opposite expressions
hand something out (9) distribute something		The teacher handed out the reading list on the first day of class. The teacher handed the reading list out on the first day of class.	Phrasal verb (trans, sep) You can *hand something out to someone,* as in *The teacher handed out the reading list to us.*	give something out pass something out	take something in keep something for oneself
have a ball (12) have a wonderful time; really enjoy oneself	informal	Hayley's party had delicious food and great music; I think the guests had a ball!		have fun have a blast/have a scream (informal) have the time of one's life (informal)	have a horrible time (informal)
have a clear conscience (2) be free of guilt		When the bank put too much money in Tony's account, he returned it because he wanted to have a clear conscience.		have clean hands (informal)	have a guilty conscience
have a lot in common (with someone) (13) be similar in many ways (to someone)		Julio and Boris have a lot in common with each other; they both like biking, roller blading, and reading.	You can substitute many other phrases for *a lot,* such as *much, quite a lot, quite a bit, something, a few things,* and *nothing.*	be a lot alike be cast in the same mold be like two peas in a pod speak the same language be birds of a feather	have nothing in common (with someone) be cast in a different mold
have got to do something (2, 14) have to do something; must do something		If Tatjana wants to stay healthy, she has got to lose weight and begin exercising.	Note that *have got to, have to,* and *must* mean the same. *Had to* is the past of all three expressions, and *will have to* is the future.	need to do something be obliged to do something	don't have to do something

Idiom and Definition	Usage	Example	Language notes	Similar expressions	Opposite expressions
have one's heart set on something (4, 8) want something very much		Gina loves literature and has her heart set on studying at Oxford next year.		set one's heart on doing something want (to do) something in the worst way (informal)	not care a bit about something not give a hoot/ damn about something (informal)
hear from someone (7, 14) receive a phone call, letter, or e-mail from someone		I heard from my brother yesterday; he called to say he was coming to town.	Phrasal verb (trans, insep)	get a call from someone be in touch with someone be in contact with someone	be out of touch with someone
help (someone) out (8) be helpful (to someone)		Can you help out my mother with that heavy box? Can you help my mother out with that heavy box?	Phrasal verb *Help out* can be intranstitive: *I'll help out.* Or, it can be transitive and separable: *I'll help you out.* Note that you can *help someone out with something,* as in the example.	lend a (helping) hand come to the aid of someone	turn your back on someone tie someone's hands
hit it off (with someone) (9) quickly become good friends (with someone)	informal	When Celia and Ivanka met on a trip to Egypt, they hit it off immediately and went everywhere together.	You can *hit it off with someone,* as in *I hit it off with Maria.*	get along well with someone take a liking to someone take a shine to someone (informal) get chummy with someone (informal)	not get along with someone be like oil and water

Idiom and Definition	Usage	Example	Language notes	Similar expressions	Opposite expressions
hit the ceiling (10) become very angry	informal	Loren hit the ceiling when she discovered that someone was stealing from her company.		lose one's temper see red (informal) hit the roof (informal) fly off the handle (informal) blow a fuse (informal) throw a fit (informal)	hold/keep one's temper calm down
hit the road (11) leave; start a trip (usually in a car)	informal	Our suitcases are packed, and we plan to hit the road right after breakfast tomorrow.		shove off push off take off get going split (slang)	stay put (informal) stick around (informal)
I'll catch you later. (7) I'll see you later.	informal	"I'll catch you later," Carlos told his daughter as he left for work.	This expression is used when leaving. *I'll* is often dropped. You can substitute future words such as *tomorrow* and *next week* for *later*.	See you later/soon. Later. (slang)	
in a flash (5) very quickly		Although I had not seen Enrique in 20 years, I recognized him in a flash.		quick as lightening in a jiffy (informal)	over a long period of time at a snail's pace
in front of someone or something (5) ahead of; before someone or something		There are large trees in front of my house.		in back of someone or something	
in the middle of something (14) while something is happening; during something		It's annoying when someone's cell phone rings in the middle of a movie.	This expression also means *in the center of,* e.g., *The park is in the middle of town.*	in the course of something	at the beginning of something at the end of something

Idiom and Definition	Usage	Example	Language notes	Similar expressions	Opposite expressions
instead of (doing) something (1) in the place of (doing) something		If you want to lose weight, you should eat fruits and vegetables instead of so many sweets.	This expression can be followed by a noun or a gerund (verb + *ing*), as in these examples: *Instead of tea, I'd like coffee, please. Instead of seeing a movie, why don't we go to a play?*	rather than something in lieu of something	in addition to something
keep a stiff upper lip (14) be brave and calm in a difficult situation		The little boy kept a stiff upper lip and didn't cry when the nurse put the needle in his arm.	When you cry, your upper lip quivers. *Keeping a stiff upper lip* refers to not crying in a difficult situation.	put up a brave front keep one's chin up bite the bullet (informal) grin and bear it (informal) keep one's cool (informal)	fall apart (at the seams) break down lose one's cool (informal)
keep in touch (with someone) (3, 12) communicate regularly (with someone)		My friend Sasha moved to Warsaw last year, but I keep in touch with him through e-mail.	*Keep in touch!* is a standard parting for friends who don't see each other very often.	stay in touch with someone stay in contact with someone maintain contact with someone	be out of touch with someone lose touch/lose contact with someone
keep someone or something away (8) make someone or something stay at a distance		Keep the baby away from the fire!	Phrasal verb (trans, sep) The object almost always separates *keep* and *away*. This expression is often followed by *from*, as in the example.	keep someone or something at arm's length hold someone off	draw someone or something close
keep someone or something out (12) not allow someone or something to enter		Shut the curtain to keep out the sun. Shut the curtain to keep the sun out.	Phrasal verb (trans, sep)		let someone or something in

Idiom and Definition	Usage	Example	Language notes	Similar expressions	Opposite expressions
keep up (with someone or something) (11) maintain the pace (of someone or something)		It's hard to keep up with new computer technology because it changes so fast.	Phrasal verb. *Keep up* is intransitive. *Keep up with* is transitive and inseparable.	keep step with someone or something keep abreast of someone or something keep pace (with someone or something)	fall behind (someone or something) lose ground (to someone or something)
lay something out (14) arrange or organize something		Tina chooses and lays out her husband's clothes every morning. Tina chooses and lays her husband's clothes out every morning.	Phrasal verb (trans, sep)		mix something up make a mess of something
let go (of someone or something) (5) release (someone or something)		When Fatma takes the children on a walk, she won't let go of their hands.	Phrasal verb (trans, insep) *Let someone go* also means *fire someone from their job.*	set someone free let something loose	get one's hands on someone or something get ahold of someone or something take hold of something hold something down
live through something (6) survive something		Mehmet lived through the earthquake, but his house was badly damaged.	Phrasal verb (trans, insep) You can *live through* such things as *a war, a difficult day, an unpleasant experience,* and *an illness.*	weather the storm (informal)	be done in by something (informal, =be defeated or killed)
look at someone or something (2) direct your eyes to someone or something		Children! Please open your books now and look at page 60 .	Phrasal verb (trans, insep)	gaze at someone or something fix one's gaze upon someone or something	look away (from someone or something) look the other way avert your eyes (from someone or something)

Idiom and Definition	Usage	Example	Language notes	Similar expressions	Opposite expressions
look for someone or something (10) try to find someone or something		Many of the original settlers of California came to look for gold.	Phrasal verb (trans, insep) You can put adverbs such as *everywhere* and *all over* between *look* and *for,* but you can't separate them with a noun or pronoun.	search for something hunt for something	track something down (=find something) come across something (=find by chance)
look forward to (doing) something (3) anticipate (doing) something with pleasure		We're looking forward to New Year's Eve and our big celebration.	Phrasal verb (trans, insep)	wait with bated breath for something be psyched for something (slang)	
look like someone or something (5) be similar in appearance to someone or something		Masaya is tall, dark, and handsome and looks like a movie star.	Often the words *just* or *exactly* occur in this expression, as in *He looks exactly like a movie star* or *He looks just like a movie star.*	look alike bear a likeness to someone be a dead ringer for someone (informal) be the spitting image of someone (informal)	look different from someone look nothing alike
lose one's cool (10) get angry; lose one's temper	informal			hit the ceiling (informal) blow a fuse (informal) fly off the handle (informal) lose it (slang)	hold one's temper keep one's cool (informal) chill out (slang)
make a trip (13) travel someplace		Khadija will make a trip to Morocco to visit her grandmother.		take a trip make a journey	stay at home stay put

Idiom and Definition	Usage	Example	Language notes	Similar expressions	Opposite expressions
make an attempt (to do something) (4) try (to do something)		Pavel said he had too much homework, but his teacher told him to make an attempt to finish it.	You can also *make an attempt at (doing) something,* as in *I'm making an attempt at organizing my desk.*	make an effort (to do something) try one's hand at something give something a try make a stab at something (informal) take a crack at something (informal) have a go at something (informal)	sit on one's hands (=do nothing)
make history (4) do something that will be remembered in history books		Charles Lindbergh made history when he flew solo across the Atlantic Ocean for the first time in 1927.		go down in history break new ground make one's mark	
make light of something (9) act as if something is unimportant		Tom was happy when he ran 2 miles, but his sister, who could run 5 miles, made light of his success.		give little weight to something attach little importance to something sneeze at something (informal) shrug something off (informal)	make a big deal out of something make a mountain out of a molehill (informal)
make plans for something (6) plan to do something		Deng bought a book about London and began to make plans for his trip.	You can also *make plans to do something,* as in *I made plans to take a trip.*	get ready to do something prepare for something cook something up (informal)	

Idiom and Definition	Usage	Example	Language notes	Similar expressions	Opposite expressions
not have a clue (7) not know anything	informal	Pietro's father doesn't have a clue about computers, so Pietro is teaching him to use the Internet.	The expression can be followed by *about something,* as in the example.	not know what's what (informal) not know the score (informal) not know up from down (informal)	know one's stuff (informal) know the ropes (informal) know the score (informal) know what's what (informal) be in the know (informal) know something inside out (=thoroughly)
not one's cup of tea (12) not something one enjoys	informal	I go to the theater alone because it's not my husband's cup of tea.		not one's thing (informal) not up one's alley (informal)	one's thing (informal) right up one's alley (informal)
on the house (2) free; paid for by the merchant		When the waiter spilled coffee on my jacket, he apologized and said dinner was on the house.	You can also say *Dinner is on us,* or *Dinner is on me.*	free of charge	
on the other hand (1) however; in contrast		Aziza keeps her office very neat, but her house, on the other hand, is a mess.		on the contrary in contrast	
on the road (11) traveling; moving from one place to another		If Rika takes the new job, she'll be on the road at least three months a year.	*On the road to something* means *progressing towards something,* as in *He's on the road to success/ recovery/ happiness.*	on one's way to a place out of town	stay at home stay put stay in the same place
one-of-a-kind (12) unique; one that does not exist elsewhere		The shopkeeper told me the necklace was one-of-a-kind, but in the next shop I saw the same thing.		out of the ordinary	run-of-the-mill

Idiom and Definition	Usage	Example	Language notes	Similar expressions	Opposite expressions
out of one's way (11) not in the direction one is going		I drove Bob home after the party even though it was out of my way.		out of the way	on one's way on the way
out of the ordinary (11) unusual; different		Those roses are out of the ordinary; I've never seen anything like them!		one-of-a-kind	run-of-the-mill
pass out (14) lose consciousness; faint		Ana was so tired after the 25 km marathon that she almost passed out.	Phrasal verb (intrans)	black out be out cold (informal) be out like a light (informal)	come to
pay for something (1) give money for something		Francois is very generous; he always pays for lunch when we eat out	Phrasal verb (trans, insep) *Pay for* can also mean *be punished for something,* as in *The criminal is paying for his crime in prison.* Note that you *pay bills, pay tuition,* and *pay rent,* but *pay for dinner, clothes, a car,* and most other things.	pick up the tab fork out money for something (slang)	
pay the price (for something)(10) receive punishment (for something)		I always pay the price for going to bed late; I'm confused and sluggish the next day.	*Pay the price for* can be followed by a noun or a gerund (verb + *ing*).	suffer the consequences of something get what's coming to you (informal) pay the piper (for something) (informal) face the music (informal) take one's medicine (informal)	get away with something go scot-free (informal) pull something off (informal)

Idiom and Definition	Usage	Example	Language notes	Similar expressions	Opposite expressions
pay through the nose (for something) (12) pay a very high price (for something)	informal	Rika loved the antique clock, and she was willing to pay through the nose for it.		pay an arm and a leg (for something) pay a fortune/ a bundle/a ton (for something)	buy something for a song pay next to nothing (for something)
plan on (doing) something (1) expect (to do) something in the future		Jose is in his third year of college and plans on graduating next year.	Phrasal verb (trans, insep)		
point something out (1) explain something; show something		During the museum tour, the guide pointed out the difference between Roman and Greek art.	Phrasal verb (trans, sep) You can *point something out to someone.*	make something clear	
pull into a place (2) arrive at a place by car, bus, or train		As the train pulled into the station, Mei saw her parents waiting on the platform.	Phrasal verb (trans, insep)	roll into a place	pull out of a place
put two and two together (14) figure something out; reason from the facts	informal	When I saw Naomi having lunch with our competitors, I put two and two together and decided she was looking for another job.		catch on (to something) get to the bottom of something puzzle something out	be in the dark not have a clue (informal) be totally clueless (slang)
put up with someone or something (3) endure or tolerate someone or something		Wilma will not put up with badly behaved children.	Phrasal verb (trans, insep)	resign oneself to something shrug something off make the best of something grin and bear it (informal)	put one's foot down (informal)

Idiom and Definition	Usage	Example	Language notes	Similar expressions	Opposite expressions
read between the lines (13) guess at something that has not been stated directly		Naomi doesn't always say what she means; you have to read between the lines.		make an inference read someone's mind	
red tape (11) unnecessary bureacratic routines		It took me 12 months to get a visa because of all the red tape.	This expression comes from the color of the tape used by government departments in England to tie up documents.		
right off the bat (2) immediately	informal	When I get up in the morning, I always drink coffee right off the bat.	This expression comes from the game of baseball: the bat is the stick you hit the ball with.	right away at once from the get-go (slang)	later on after a while
rip something off / rip someone off (7) steal something/ steal from someone	slang or informal	Someone ripped off my bag. Someone ripped my bag off. Someone ripped me off.	Phrasal verb (trans, sep) You can *rip off a person, a thing, or a place. The boys ripped off the store* means that they stole something from the store.		
run into someone or something (11) meet someone or something unexpectedly		I was so surprised to run into Jaime yesterday; I hadn't seen him in years!	Phrasal verb (trans, insep) *Run into something* can also mean *crash into something,* as in *He lost control of the car and ran into a tree.*	bump into someone or something	steer clear of someone or something (= avoid)

Idiom and Definition	Usage	Example	Language notes	Similar expressions	Opposite expressions
search for someone or something (6) look everywhere for someone or something		Iris searched everywhere for her glasses and finally found them under the bed.	Phrasal verb (trans, insep) You can put adverbs such as *everywhere, hard,* and *all over* between *search* and *for,* but you can't separate these words with a noun or pronoun.	hunt for someone or something search high and low for something (= search everywhere)	give up the search for someone or something
see red (10) be very angry	informal	I see red when people throw trash out of car windows.	This expression comes from the fact that when bulls see red they become angry.	be mad as hell/as a hornet (informal) be fuming (informal) be steaming/ steamed (informal) get hot under the collar (informal) hit the ceiling/roof (informal)	calm down keep one's cool (informal)
set eyes on someone or something (13) see someone or something for the first time		When Lucia first set eyes on the lovely Pacific coast, she wanted to stay there forever.	Although this expression already means *see for the first time,* the word *first* is often placed in front of it for extra emphasis, as in the example.	lay eyes on someone or something	
set one's sights on (doing) something (4) choose (to do) something as a goal		The company set its sights on becoming the world's largest provider of computer software.		aim for something	give up on (doing) something

Idiom and Definition	Usage	Example	Language notes	Similar expressions	Opposite expressions
set out (on a hike, a walk, a trip) (5) begin (a hike, a walk, a trip)		When we set out, the weather was fine, but later it started to rain. When we set out on the walk, the weather was fine.	Phrasal verb *Set out* is intransitive. *Set out on* is transitive and inseparable.	start out (on a walk, a hike, a trip) take off (on a trip) get going (informal)	wrap up a trip come home go back/come back
settle down (11) begin to live a stable life in one place		Tim and Maya decided to settle down and have a family.	Phrasal verb (intrans) You can *settle down with someone, settle down in a place,* and *settle down and do something* (get married, have a family, etc.) This expression can also mean *calm down,* as in *Children, you're too noisy. Settle down!*		sow one's wild oats (=do wild things in one's youth) live on the edge live out of a suitcase
show up (at a place)(8, 9) arrive (somewhere); appear		We waited and waited for our teacher. Finally, she showed up a half hour late.	Phrasal verb (intrans)	turn up	vanish into thin air (=disappear) go away take off (=leave)
sleep on it (2) decide later, often the next day	informal	I'm not sure if I should accept that job offer. I'll have to sleep on it.		spend time thinking about something	make a split-second decision decide then and there (=decide immediately)
soul mate (1) perfect life partner		When Gina met Miguel, she knew he was her soul mate; they loved the same books, the same movies, and the same sports.		true love heart's desire	complete opposite

Idiom and Definition	Usage	Example	Language notes	Similar expressions	Opposite expressions
spend time doing something (3, 10, 11) use time to do something		I'd like to spend time working in the garden today.	Phrases indicating quantity such as *a lot of, a little,* and *quite a bit of* can occur with this expression, as in *She spends a lot of time cooking for her family.*	take time to do something	not have time to do something take time off from doing something
sure enough (7) as expected	informal	Zoran thought he had done well on the test and, sure enough, he made an A.		wouldn't you know it (informal) lo and behold (informal) sure as shooting (slang)	much to one's surprise to one's amazement
take a shower/bath (3) wash yourself in the shower or bath		I usually take a shower in the evening.		have a shower/bath	
take a stand (3) clearly and loudly declare your point of view		Mimi realized her company was polluting the city's water supply, and she decided it was time to take a stand.	You can *take a stand for* or *against* something, as in *We need to take a stand for clean air* and *We must take a stand against pollution.*	take a position take sides defend your position stick up for your guns (informal, = defend your position)	be non-commital go back and forth on an issue sit/be/stay on the fence (informal) be wishy-washy (informal) blow hot and cold (informal)
take ages (13) take a long time	informal	It takes ages to send a letter through the post office; why don't you just e-mail or fax me?	*Ages* means *a long time* and also occurs in the following expressions: *for ages, it's been ages, in ages.*	take forever take a coon's age (informal)	take just a moment/a minute

Idiom and Definition	Usage	Example	Language notes	Similar expressions	Opposite expressions
take place (9) happen		The celebration will take place at 10 a.m. at Perez Park.			be cancelled/be called off be postponed/be put off
take something off (12, 14) remove something (clothing, jewelry, makeup, a cover from a jar, etc.)		Misha took off his coat and threw it on the chair. Misha took his coat off and threw it on the chair.	Phrasal verb **(trans, sep)**		put something on
take something out (1) remove something		Children, please take out your workbooks from your desks! Children, please take your workbooks out of your desks!	Phrasal verb (trans, sep) Note how *from* and *of* are used in the examples.	get something out	put something in
That's the last straw! (10) After so many problems, that's just too much to endure!	informal	Doris was often late to work, but when she missed the annual meeting, it was the last straw. Her boss fired her.	This expression refers to the image of a camel being loaded with straw. The load becomes heavier and heavier until one straw becomes too much and the camel's back breaks.	That's the straw that broke the camel's back. That's the limit! That takes the cake! I've had it! That does it!	
the first leg (14) the first part of a trip		The first leg of our bike trip was hard because we were out of shape, but it got easier.		the first stretch	the last leg the home stretch
the last leg (11) the final stage of a trip		Our trip was great for the most part, but I got sick on the last leg.		the home stretch	the first leg the first stretch

Idiom and Definition	Usage	Example	Language notes	Similar expressions	Opposite expressions
think about someone or something (6) remember; consider someone or something		I'm thinking about dinner; what would you like to eat?	Phrasal verb (trans, insep) *Think about* can be followed by a noun, as in the example, or a gerund (verb + *ing*), as in *I'm thinking about cooking dinner.*	think something over daydream about someone or something	not give someone or something a second thought
tie the knot (with someone) (9) marry (someone)	informal	Roberto and Berta finally tied the knot after living together for 10 years.	The subject is usually plural, as in *We tied the knot; They tied the knot.*	get married (to someone) get hitched (informal)	get divorced get a divorce break up split up (informal)
to the letter (14) exactly as written or instructed; perfectly		The employees carried out their boss's orders to the letter.	This expression is an adverbial phrase that tells *how*. It often occurs in phrases such as *follow the instructions to the letter, carry out the plan to the letter.*	to a T (informal) to a turn	
wake up (12) awaken from sleep		I woke up in the middle of the night when the storm started.	Phrasal verb (intrans) However, *wake someone up* is transitive and separable and means *cause someone to awaken,* as in *I woke Maria up at 6:00 a.m. so she could catch a plane.*		go to sleep fall asleep nod off doze off go to the land of Nod (informal)

Idiom and Definition	Usage	Example	Language notes	Similar expressions	Opposite expressions
what if (1) what will happen if		What if there's an earthquake? Will these buildings stand or collapse?	In very formal English, the example would be stated *What if there were an earthquake? Would these buildings stand or collapse?*	suppose that let's say that (informal)	
why in the world? (14) why really? why in fact?	informal	Why in the world are those children making so much noise?	The phrase *in the world* is used to show strong feelings or surprise. Other expressions are *how in the world?, where in the world?, who in the world?,* and *what in the world?*	why on earth? (informal)	why in the world not? why on earth not?
year after year (6) regularly for many years		You've had the Christmas party at your house year after year; aren't you tired of the responsibility?		year in and year out day after day week after week month after month	once in a blue moon (informal, = very rarely)
year in and year out (4) continuously for years		Every summer, year in and year out, we go to the same beach resort, and I never get tired of it!	The expression can also be stated *year in, year out.*	year after year day in, day out week in, week out	once in a blue moon (informal, = very rarely)